Chosen

Building Your Family the Way God Builds His

Andrew Hopper

New Growth Press, Greensboro, NC 27401
Newgrowthpress.com

Cover Design: Faceout Studio, faceoutstudio.com
Interior Typesetting and Ebook: Lisa Parnell, lparnellbookservices.com

ISBN: 978-1-64507-572-1 (paperback)
ISBN: 978-1-64507-573-8 (ebook)

Library of Congress Cataloging-in-Publication Data on file

Printed in Colombia

30 29 28 27 26 1 2 3 4 5

"This book builds the biblical foundation for adoption for all of us who follow Christ and have been chosen by God. It is honest in how challenging adoption can be, and it sets a vision for the impact adoptive parents and local churches can have in the lives of children and communities."

Bryant Wright, Former Pastor of Johnson Ferry Baptist Church; founder, Right From The Heart Ministries

"Andrew Hopper's book is a timely reminder of how the body of Christ is uniquely equipped to care for vulnerable members of the adoption kinship network. A must-read for prospective adoptive parents, foster parents, and support networks."

Rebekah McGee, LMSW, Adjunct Professor, The University of Alabama School of Social Work; birth parent/adoption social worker; adoptive parent

"Biblical, gospel-centered, and deeply practical—this book takes a powerful look at adoption and the church's role in serving the vulnerable. It offers a clear call to action and spiritual growth. The Hoppers' testimony inspires, and I'm grateful to have Andrew as my pastor and example in this mission."

David Melber, President and CEO, Baptist Children's Homes of North Carolina; adoptive father

"We adopted three kids from three different countries, and the gospel principles Andrew speaks to in this book are the ones that inspired and sustained us in answering the call to adopt. *Chosen* does not sugarcoat the challenges adoption brings, but it provides wisdom that will help guide you and your family."

Kevin Ezell, President, North American Mission Board, SBC

"The gospel compels us to care for the orphan, and adoption invites not only families but entire communities to be the hands and feet of Christ. In *Chosen*, Andrew Hopper exhorts believers to consider adoption, and he is honest about its challenges while pointing to God's faithful presence."

Todd Unzicker, Executive Director-Treasurer, North Carolina Baptists

"Andrew Hopper has a prophetic gift wedded to a pastor's heart. The stories in *Chosen* will not only warm your heart, they'll compel you to get involved in the incredible ministry of adoption. As Andrew shows us, the gospel is the source of it all. Enthusiastically recommended!"

J. D. Greear, Lead Pastor, The Summit Church, Raleigh-Durham, NC

"Adoption is at the heart of the gospel of Jesus Christ. This book is both a reminder of the intentional Father we have in God and the great lengths he has gone in order to make us sons and daughters in his family. This is a book you read, then you go and live differently. Let's go!"

Ryan Britt, Executive Ministries Pastor, The Church of Eleven22

"*Chosen* is a book on adoption grounded in the beautiful truth of the believer's adoption into the family of God through faith in Jesus Christ. This message is biblical, practical, and inspirational. Every pastor who wants to cultivate a culture of adoption in his own church should read this book."

Daniel L. Akin, President, Judson College/Southeastern Baptist Theological Seminary, Wake Forest, NC

"Adoption is not first a human idea but God's idea, rooted in his eternal plan of love. Andrew reminds us that the gospel doesn't motivate us with guilt but with grace. This book will encourage families, equip churches, and most of all, exalt the God who makes orphans his sons and daughters."

Tony Merida, Pastor, Imago Dei Church, Raleigh, NC; vice president, Send Network

TO HJ, AP, AND DB.

Your mother and I see the unconditional love
and unending patience you have with us and your sister.
We are all so much better for it.

Contents

Foreword

Back in the 1970s–80s, I was in elementary school, excelling in building forts and digging foxholes on the farm with my friends. My family had two items of advanced technology: a cordless phone and a Polaroid camera. That camera was well used. The house was full of pictures of our family.

One of those Polaroid pictures was taken in the backyard. I was probably two years old and was in the kiddie pool while my parents and grandparents sat in folding chairs talking. I still don't know who took that picture, but I know that I took it to show and tell at Shannon Forest Elementary School.

As I showed the picture to my class and told the story of how my mama and daddy adopted me because they couldn't have children, the big bully in my class spoke up. He had a beard and drove himself to elementary school. He'd been held back a few times and was twice our size (that's how I remember him, anyway).

He said, "You must have been the ugliest baby ever born if your own mom looked at you and didn't want you."

The class laughed in unison, and I felt my heart fill with something worse than shame. For the first time in my life, I wondered if I should have never been born.

When my mom picked me up from school that day she knew, like mamas know, that I was upset, so she asked me, "Who did it?"

When I told her what the big bully in the first-grade class said to me, she spent a minute telling me all the ways she would get revenge on him and his family. Then as she calmed down, she slowly explained to me the significance of being adopted. This is pretty close to verbatim:

> "Your daddy and I prayed for you for ten years before you became our son. Way before you were born, we asked the Lord for a boy, and he answered our prayer by giving us you. We adopted you three months after you were born, and you became a part of our family. And we're praying that one day soon, Jesus will adopt you, and you'll become a part of his family too."

My mom did something on the ride home that day that literally changed the course of my life. She connected my adoption to the gospel. My parents' prayers were answered, and I did join the family of God when I was fourteen years old.

When I became a Christian, I had a fuller understanding of the gospel, because I knew what it meant to be adopted—to be invited and welcomed in to a relationship based only on the love and grace of the one extending the invitation.

When Andrew told me about this book, the hair on my arms stood up. I felt the tangible presence of the Holy Spirit as I imagined how many people would be encouraged and inspired and challenged by the story of the Hopper family.

Andrew doesn't paint a rosy picture of adoption—he paints a real one. It's a different kind of difficult. It's unpredictable and surprising and maddening and amazing. And all of it is a reflection of the gospel—the story of how God adopted us into his family through the death and resurrection of his own Son, Jesus Christ.

You'll appreciate the fact that this book is not a guilt-laden sales pitch to get you to foster or adopt kids. There's none of that here. Just a raw and hopeful story of pain and peace, of hardship and happiness, and all the surprising ways a family comes together to open their arms and their hearts to a new member.

Clayton King
President, Clayton King Ministries
Evangelist, Pastor, Husband, Daddy, Son

Introduction

First, I want to say, Breathe easy! I know talking about adoption can bring up all types of pressure. Let's try to take the air out of that balloon from the jump. Guilt and pressure can surround young Christian couples when the subject of adoption is broached. And the subject comes up a lot nowadays!

Thankfully, adoption is more of an open conversation now than it was a generation ago. I am a millennial, but more like a geriatric millennial. I remember drinking Crystal Pepsi, dying of dysentery on the Oregon Trail video game, and reading books to earn a Personal Pan Pizza from Pizza Hut! I was raised in a good church with godly parents. Adoption certainly wasn't demeaned, but it also wasn't discussed. That has really changed, and may God be glorified for it! Church ministries and books have helped put Christian adoption more front and center in our current age. All these things are good! But they can also create pressure and guilt as families and churches begin to touch on this important topic.

So let me just say it plainly: Not everyone is called to adoption. The primary objective in this book is not to guilt more Christians into adopting children. Instead of guilt, the object is awe. Every Christian knows what it means to be adopted. Every Christian was lost without hope before they met Christ. They were orphaned before God stepped into their life and restored them to his family. If you are a Christian, you are adopted into the family of God. Remembering the gospel results in a passion that guilt can't touch. Guilt is akin to putting fire under someone. Sure, it gets them moving, but when the heat is gone, all forward progress will stop. The gospel is a different motivation. The gospel puts fire *in* someone rather than under them. That is the aim of this book.

Rather than guilting people into adoption, I hope to awaken them to their own spiritual adoption. Our hearts will burn with passion for others only after we understand God's passion for us. That is the fuel we need to walk the long road of adoption and support others who do the same.

Outside of marriage, adoption is the single greatest metaphor for God's work in our lives. Romans 8 describes God choosing us: "You have received the Spirit of adoption as sons, by whom we cry, 'Abba! Father!' The Spirit himself bears witness with our spirit that we are children of God" (Romans 8:15–16). Despite our flaws and rebellion, God *chose* us to be part of his family. His Spirit also reminds us of who we are as adopted children. This truth naturally leads many Christians to adopt, and it encourages all Christians to support those who do. The gospel is different; it changes everything. The gospel takes us farther than guilt because it weaves the title of "chosen" into our identity. Subsequently, that identity comes out in our everyday lives. Chosen people choose people. When we adopt, we are building our families the way God builds his.

My hope is for this message to become central in your adoption journey. That journey for you may be adopting. Or maybe your journey will be holding the rope to support adoptive families. In either case, you will need the gospel as fuel for that mission. As an adoptive father of a special needs child, I know firsthand how badly you need the fire in you rather than under you. I hope this book forms a vital stepping stone in your journey.

1

The Story of Adoption

Adoption is hard. Trust me, because I know. We adopted our daughter, Faith Ann, into our family in 2017. After we did, my wife didn't sleep through the night for the next four years. We could literally count on two hands the number of nights she didn't have to get up with Faith Ann during this time. Nights were plagued by gastrostomy tube (G-tube) feedings, diaper changes, constant sickness, and the general unrest often associated with Down syndrome. Adoption is on the front lines of spiritual warfare. When you sign up for war, I promise you'll need more than a cute picture and a sad story. The cute picture crashes against a rock of reality. And when you get tired enough, that sad story doesn't seem sad enough.

So when it comes to the "why" of adoption, cute pictures and sad stories are out. What about gut-wrenching statistics? These are not good enough reasons to adopt either. At any given time, there are well over half a million kids in foster care in the United States. Half of them do not exit the system in the same year they enter it, and among that group, half are waiting for adoption because parental rights have been terminated with no hope for reunification.[1] Where I live and minister, in the Triad region of North Carolina, two thousand kids enter the foster care system each year.[2] Neglect and drug abuse make up 90 percent of the causes for placement.[3] There are over fifteen million double orphans (children who have lost both parents) worldwide.[4] Finally, there are over eight hundred thousand abortions in the United States every single year, and this is after the overturning of *Roe v. Wade.*

The statistics are staggering, and I could go on and on. However, the numbers alone are not sufficient reasons to personally enter this ministry. They are great reasons to pray, raise awareness, and support others. But at the end of the day, when adoption becomes personally challenging, large cultural trends—as sad as they are—won't matter much.

Let me illustrate. One afternoon when our adopted daughter Faith Ann was a few years old, I walked in the front door to pure and utter chaos. My three eldest children were crying, and my wife looked extremely scared. Faith Ann had just had a seizure. She was three years old, but as a child with Down syndrome, she weighed only about fifteen pounds. In the ambulance, her heart rate was over 200 beats per minute. It was all terribly scary, and it happened extremely fast. As I drove to the hospital that night, I promise you that the plight of orphans worldwide was not on my mind. Neither was fatherlessness or the foster system. Cute pictures, sad stories, and gut-wrenching statistics are not good enough reasons to adopt. Adoption requires a great reason, not simply a good one. The emotional, financial, and spiritual hardships that accompany adoption render a good reason insufficient. Praise God that we have a great reason in the gospel.

CONSIDER YOUR ADOPTION

If good reasons are not enough to adopt, why should Christians choose to build families through adoption? That really is the bottom-line question. Our commitment to adoption cannot rise above our "why." And our deepest answer to "why" doesn't come from thinking about someone else's need for physical adoption; it comes from thinking about our own need for spiritual adoption. Our awe over God adopting us pushes us to think about adopting others. We needed spiritual adoption, and God sent Jesus Christ to do everything necessary to adopt us. Simply put, the gospel compels us to enter the spiritual battle of adoption.

The gospel produces awe in the children of God, which sustains us when things get hard. This is where we must start. The Bible says we were orphans. We were estranged from God, our Father, because of sin. But he came for us, chose us, rescued us, restored us, and reconciled us. He adopted us. We must remember this truth in all its wonder and stoke the kindling of these embers until they whip into a flame.

Returning to the gospel can sometimes elicit an eye roll from Christians. At other times, it may provoke a yawn. Even something as beautiful as the gospel can become so familiar to us that we fail to be continually moved by it. A few years ago, I was in Peru sharing Bible stories as we helped an indigenous farmer plant coffee beans. I will never forget standing on the edge of a jungle mountain gazing across a picturesque valley toward another towering mountain range. The sun was rising over the peaks and lighting up the sky. I stood there in amazement with my mouth wide open, barely able to look down. Yet the farmer I was helping hadn't even bothered to look up! We can all become immune to things, no matter how beautiful or valuable they are.

The gospel is a beautiful thing of immense value. In fact, the Bible likens it to treasure hidden in a field, worth trading everything in our lives to possess. However, if we're not careful, we can become desensitized to its significance. We need to awaken from our slumber and behold the gospel in all its beauty and fullness. We won't adopt unless we are in awe.

STAND IN AWE OVER YOUR ADOPTION

In 1 John 2–3, God calls us his children—a truth that should take our breath away! Consider 2:28–29:

> And now, little children, abide in him, so that when he appears we may have confidence and not shrink from him in shame at his coming. If you know that he is righteous, you may be sure that everyone who practices righteousness has been born of him.

This passage becomes clear when viewed through the lens of a father's relationship with his children. When children see their father, they typically have one of two reactions: They either step forward with confidence or shrink back in shame. The determining factor is often the kind of day the children have had. I experienced this when my own children were little. Upon hearing, "Daddy's home!" they would be filled with excitement and rush out to greet me and play. That is, of course, unless they had gotten in trouble that day. If they were in trouble, they would shrink back rather than approach with full confidence.

Whenever my children didn't come running out, I would inevitably ask, "What happened?" On one occasion, it turned out that one brother had hit the other in the head with a golf club! No wonder they didn't come out to greet me. Their reaction to my presence had much to do with how they felt about their behavior. The Bible says in Romans 3 and 6 that all have sinned and the penalty for our sin is death. Every errant thought, manifestation of pride, and hurtful word places us in a posture of shame rather than confidence. Yet, we see in 1 John 2 that we can experience joy in the presence of our heavenly Father. How can this be?

The answer is found in one little word: *abide*. We are instructed in 1 John 2:28 to abide in him so that we may have confidence in his presence. Abiding—remaining in Christ—produces confidence in God's presence. In contrast, failing to abide results in shame at his coming. To "abide in him" means to remain, to live in, to dwell in the daily reality of your relationship with Christ and your dependence on him.

John also talks about this in chapter 15 of his gospel, where he records Jesus's striking analogy of a branch and a vine to illustrate what it means to follow him: "Abide in me, and I in you. As the branch cannot bear fruit by itself, unless it abides in the vine, neither can you, unless you abide in me" (John 15:4).

It's helpful to have this metaphor in mind as John brings the language back in 1 John. He instructs children to abide in Jesus, or, as seen in John 15, to remain in the vine. If you want to grow and bear fruit, you must be in the vine. Similarly, if you want to be confident at the Lord's coming, abide in him. Our confidence before the Lord stems (pardon the pun) from being found in the vine and united to Jesus. If our confidence were based on our works, we would never run outside when our heavenly Father pulls into the driveway! But being in the vine means that God has covered our sin in Christ and that we are part of his family. What incredible news that is for all sinners!

The realization that we are children of God culminates in what commentators identify as an emotional outburst from John (and hopefully us): "See what kind of love the Father has given to us, that we should be called children of God; and so we are" (1 John 3:1). John is certainly having a moment here. The phrase, "see what kind of love the Father has given to us," is an ecstatic emotional expression. He is overwhelmed by a truth that should overwhelm all of us. John doesn't just understand what God has done for him; he feels it!

Chapter 2 of 1 John ends by stating the facts of our adoption into God's family, and chapter 3 begins with the emotions that should follow those facts. Think about marriage, for example. You could get married simply by quietly signing the license at a courthouse. But marriage usually sparks a celebration, complete with a wedding ceremony, vows, a reception, and the joy of sharing the moment with friends and family. There is a legal side and an emotional side to marriage.

Like John, we should want our emotions to fall in line with our knowledge. So don't just graduate from high school—throw your cap! Don't just receive salvation—celebrate it! See what kind of love the Father has given to us. Behold it. See it, and savor it. Drink it in. Pause and look at it with wonder and awe. When John says, "what kind of love," he is using a figure of speech that literally means, "What country is this from?" It's similar to when we ask, "Where did that come from?" The love from God wasn't deserved, but it was given anyway. In fact, the New International Version puts it beautifully: "See what great love the Father has lavished on us, that we should be called children of God!" (1 John 3:1).

Although we don't deserve our place in God's family, every Christian has it. Here we are. Our status is not because of anything we did right, but because of his love that he lavished upon us. The reality of the new birth stirs affection in us for our heavenly Father. That is certainly what is happening here with John. Does it happen in your life? I don't mean every day or on command, but at times the facts of the gospel should overwhelm us. We should stand in awe over our adoption and feel the weight of what God did for us.

It's like a child being caught in his father's arms, feeling the love they already know. I've reflected on this many times with my own children. When I'm tender with them and hold them, they experience something from me that they instinctively understand. Picking up a child doesn't tell them something they don't already know. But it helps them to feel it.

Experiencing God's love up close pushes us to adoption. Adopted people adopt people. Why do we build our families through adoption? We do it because we are building our families the way God built his.

REFLECTION QUESTIONS

- Before reading this chapter, what main motivations did you have in either pursuing adoption or supporting it?
- How do you think the gospel story ties into adoption?
- How does thinking about your own spiritual adoption make you feel?

2

Our Story of Adoption

~

As a result of God's love in adopting us, our family stepped into adoption in 2017.

I'll never forget where I was when I received the call that Faith Ann was born. It was already an exciting day because my two older kids and I were going to pick up two pigs to add to our little farm. Of course, my kids didn't know that. I told them we needed the horse trailer because I was picking up some furniture. Somewhere between Summerfield and Asheboro, North Carolina, my phone rang. I received the news that Faith Ann had been born, and her mother wanted to move forward with placing her in our home!

The adoption agency we worked with made a point of always calling the adoptive dad first. They said adoptive moms get too emotional and forget details in moments like this (their words, not mine!). So, it was up to me to call Anna and share the news. When I told Anna, we both cried on the phone. Then I realized my older daughter was listening to the whole thing. She was only seven, but she was as sharp as a tack and understood everything that was happening. So now the three of us were crying and praising God for Faith Ann's healthy birth.

Then Anna asked me, "Well, what are y'all going to do?"

"What do you mean?" I replied.

"Well, we have to be in Raleigh-Durham in the morning, and we have a million things to do! Are y'all going to come home?"

"Yeah, babe, we are going to come home," I replied, "right after I pick up these pigs!" We were adding to the family this particular weekend in more ways than one!

A WELCOME SURPRISE

If it seems like Faith Ann's birth caught us a little bit off guard, that's because it absolutely did. About a month before she was born, our adoption agency gave us some news. They didn't use loaded language or make things more emotional than necessary, but the fact was, a mother had chosen our profile, and her baby had a 99 percent chance of having Down syndrome. This was obviously a major curveball. After the call, we sat in silence for a few minutes. The agency advised us not to make a decision right away; they wanted us to take a few days to pray and process everything. We wanted to honor their advice, so we committed the next few days to praying.

It was much more emotional than I anticipated. From the first moment of the call, I think Anna and I both knew we were going to say yes. However, the weight of what that decision meant began to sink in as we learned more about Down syndrome. Over the next few days, we had countless conversations, engaged in research, met with our family doctor to ask questions, and talked to friends and family.

We discovered that Down syndrome covers a broad spectrum. Some individuals with Down syndrome grow up to have fairly typical lives, while others may never talk or walk. There's no way to predict how it will play out. In any case, life expectancy is generally lower, intellectual disabilities are common, and there are numerous health challenges associated with the syndrome. A significant amount of therapy and medical care is often required.

A few things stand out in my mind from those days. The first standout moment was a conversation I had with my father. I grew up in a blue-collar family—my mother worked faithfully at a law office, and my dad built houses and drove trucks. But after I went to college, he began working as an aide in a special needs classroom and quickly fell in love with the kids and the job. Ultimately, he chose to earn his degree specifically to work with this population. Looking back, we can see how God was preparing so many things for our special girl years in advance!

I was anxious to talk with my dad because of his experience. We discussed what adopting a special needs child might look like, and he asked me what we were going to do. Although I thought I knew, I told him we were praying about it. His response shocked me: "What is there to pray about?" The situation seemed straightforward to him. We prayed, felt called, and asked God to give us an adopted child. A birth mom chose us to be the parents of her precious baby. It seemed to my dad that God had already answered our prayers!

The second standout event happened when Anna and I were taking the kids to see a circus (one with elephants!). I was coming from the church office, and Anna and I were talking on the phone as I drove to meet them. When the conversation turned to the adoption, Anna told me that she felt like God could do anything.

She had confidence that God would sustain us through whatever challenges this little girl faced. When I hung up the phone, the Lord spoke to me. I don't throw that phrase around lightly. I believe the Bible is the Word of God, and I see no New Testament examples of people asking God to speak to them. However, God can do whatever he wants to do! All the Lord said to me in this moment was, "Her name is Faith." That was enough to break my heart for this child, and in that moment, the decision was made for me.

We called the adoption agency and gave them our yes. They were thrilled and set up a meeting a few days later for us to meet with Faith Ann's birth mom. However, the night before the meeting was supposed to occur, the agency representative called us to let us know that Faith Ann's birth mom had stopped communicating with them, and they were unsure the meeting would take place. It was disheartening, but we tried not to read too much into it. More days passed, and still no one heard from the mom. We were told the chances of this adoption being completed were slim.

Anna and I were both pretty sad, but we fought to remember that this was all in God's hands. Days turned into a week, and a week turned into multiple weeks. It began to seem like it wasn't in God's plan for this little girl to join our family. It was hard for me to reconcile that thought with hearing the Lord's voice. While I didn't have a specific promise, I had the feeling that somehow this would work out. And, by God's grace, that's what happened. In his perfect timing, Faith Ann's mom reached out to the agency, and Faith Ann was born on the same day. It was wild.

A LOOK BACK

On our drive to Raleigh to meet Faith Ann and her birth mom, we spent some time reflecting on our journey. This adoption process had been long and filled with ups and downs. Each of us had a heart for adoption that began independently during our younger years on the mission field. Anna served in East Asia, and I spent every summer from ages twelve to twenty-two on Native American reservations in Montana. Both of us had seen the plight of children growing up in unbelieving homes and that of many kids facing tough situations. Additionally, Anna always had a special place in her heart for those with special needs. She was drawn to them, and they were drawn to her.

During our engagement, we talked about having kids and knew we shared a desire to adopt. A couple of years into our marriage, we moved to Wake Forest, North Carolina, so I could pursue a Master of Divinity at Southeastern Baptist Theological Seminary. We attended The Summit Church and were drawn again to adoption through our friendship with a family embarking on their second international adoption and the preaching ministry of J. D. Greear.

Anna and I decided to pursue adoption and having biological children simultaneously. We were leaving things in God's hands. We went through the foster system and got licensed with the hope of fostering to adopt. During that time, Anna became pregnant but unfortunately miscarried the child. The Lord healed our broken hearts, and he kept our focus on him.

Being licensed foster parents gave us valuable insight into the system. Our social worker was fantastic, but she was also juggling dozens of families with kids in very tough situations. Years later, this experience influences the way our church seeks to support these workers through our Chosen ministry. Anna and I were licensed for a year, but ultimately, we never received a placement. There were a few starts and stops, including a call around the time our oldest daughter, HattieJo, was born. That was quite a surprise—we thought we were going from zero to two kids just like that! But it wasn't meant to be.

When HattieJo was born, we decided to pause our adoption plans for a season and revisit them in a few years. This decision seemed wise, especially as we were preparing to plant Mercy Hill, the church I now pastor. Those years were incredibly fast-paced and chaotic! However, around 2014, we began to gradually revisit the adoption conversation, and we resumed the adoption process in 2016.

Although we had completed all the paperwork for adoption, we hadn't yet committed to the full financial obligation. While we didn't need to provide the money immediately, we needed to be prepared to cover costs at any moment a placement occurred. I vividly remember Anna and I praying together in our kitchen. It was a true crisis-of-faith moment. We held hands over the kitchen table, making the decision to proceed despite not knowing how we would manage financially. We had just increased our giving at church and had invested almost everything we had into building our homestead. Despite these challenges, we felt strongly that God was directing us in this path, and we trusted in his provision. Besides, we figured we wouldn't get a placement for another year or so, right? Well, Faith Ann was born just a month and a half later!

All this was running through our minds on the drive to Raleigh, as we imagined what it would be like to meet Faith Ann and her mom. It felt like a long road, but in reality, our journey was just about to begin. Looking back, that entire day was a whirlwind. It was emotional and positive. Meeting Faith Ann was one of the most impactful moments of my life. I was overwhelmed with love for her. Although she had no biological connection to our family, I felt that God honored our commitment to her by filling us with a profound love for her.

As I mentioned before, Faith Ann was tiny—so tiny that Anna described her as "T-tiny." She was also in the neonatal intensive care unit due to Down syndrome, a heart defect, and feeding difficulties. What we initially thought might be just a few nights in the NICU stretched into a couple of months. It was a challenging time. Early on, we were informed that Faith Ann would need open-heart surgery but would first need to gain weight. Unfortunately, she struggled with bottle feeding and had to be placed on a feeding tube. The goal was for her to bottle-feed before going home. However, not being at home kept her in an environment that wasn't ideal for resting and growing, which might have helped with her feeding issues.

Anna was an absolute rock during this time. She was at home with us and at the hospital with Faith Ann every single day, despite the 1.5-hour drive. About a month in, we decided to transfer Faith Ann to a hospital about thirty-five minutes from our house. Soon the doctors at the new hospital believed that getting her home would be the best for her holistic health and put her on a G-tube so that we could feed her from home. It turned out to be the right call. Two months after she was born, Faith Ann came home on April 6, 2017. She still weighed about five pounds, but wouldn't you know it, the very night she came home she drank about half a bottle by herself!

One of the sweetest memories I have from this time is how quickly our other children took to Faith Ann. They loved her as a full sibling from the start. Their lives were turned upside down, but they adapted remarkably well, and we settled into life with a special child. This included countless therapy appointments, meetings, and explaining to others why she is unique. We all understood that God had entrusted our entire family with the stewardship of this precious gift. Although this gift came with sacrifices, our children have never, not once, complained about the demands on their time. Their love for Faith Ann has been a testament to God's love for us, reflected in how we love one another.

Our extended family's acceptance of Faith Ann is also a testimony of God's love. They supported us throughout the entire adoption process in countless ways, and when Faith Ann came home, they embraced her as a full member of the family. Both Anna and I are blessed to come from a godly heritage. Faith Ann has two sets of grandparents, along with aunts and uncles, who are all eager to help in any way they can.

On March 7, 2018, we received Faith Ann's adoption decree. It was an incredible day. While she had already been functioning as a full member of the family, the adoption decree made it official. Faith Ann became a forever Hopper.

REFLECTION QUESTIONS

- What parts of our story do you personally connect with?
- Do any parts of our story surprise you? If so, why?
- Does any specific Scripture come to mind as you read our story? If so, why do you think the Lord might be bringing those verses to you now?

3

The Motivation for Adoption

Several families in our church have given up their early empty-nest years to adopt middle schoolers from the foster system. They traded financial freedom and available time to take on children with significant trauma from tumultuous pasts. A decision like this isn't made lightly, and it is a lifelong commitment. Why would anyone do this? They did it because the gospel compelled them. Christians need a great reason to walk the road of adoption. Adoption is joyful, but it is also hard. As Elisabeth Elliot said, "It is impossible to love deeply without sacrifice."[1]

In adoption, we bring children into our homes who often carry familial, relational, and medical brokenness. Cute pictures, sad stories, and heartbreaking statistics are not strong enough reasons to walk this road. Another tempting reason to pursue adoption is also insufficient: If we aren't careful, we can end up adopting *for* God's love rather than *from* it. This is problematic for at least two reasons.

First, that's just not the gospel. It may be religion, but it's not the gospel. The gospel isn't an invitation to work hard and make yourself acceptable to God. Rather, it assumes that the very notion of working for our salvation is dismissed. Ephesians 2:8–9 is as plain as it gets: Salvation is by grace through faith in Christ alone. Much of the New Testament was written to address churches dealing with heretics who were trying to add works into the mix. Our salvation rests solely on the life, death, burial, and resurrection of Christ. When we put our faith in him, his blood covers our sin, and God counts us sinless because of Christ. There are many forms of works-based righteousness in our land. Whether it's served up southern-fried or northern-steamed, it's false doctrine. Some people can grow up in church their entire lives and come away with the message, "Don't drink, cuss, smoke, or chew, or date girls who do, and God will accept you!" I'm being a bit humorous here, but really, any type of moral fruit could go on that list. Be generous, don't sleep around, or even adopt children so that God will love you. What a tragedy. That message is the direct opposite of the gospel. God didn't accept us because we were acceptable; he accepts us because Jesus was acceptable and stepped into our place. We don't adopt to be spiritually adopted; we adopt because God adopted us.

Second, adopting for God's love naturally sets up a transactional relationship between parents and adopted children. If we believe that our behavior determines whether God loves us, won't we treat our children the same way? Imagine an adopted child (or any child) who constantly feels pressure to be valuable just to stay in their family. How sad would that be? They take out the trash, do the dishes, and desperately try to stay out of the other children's way. When asked why they work so hard and never relax, their response might be, "I am hoping you will accept me!" In other words, their response is, "I fear you will reject me!" In this scenario, obedience is based on the inferior motive of fear. When the fear ends, the conformity will stop. Fear is a potent motivator for a time, and it can even make us moral for a while. But in the end, fear is only capable of producing mechanical change.

Think about a metal bar. If you apply enough pressure, you can bend it. But if you ever remove the pressure, it will snap right back into its former position.[2] That's how we can be when we are motivated by fear. The change isn't produced from the heart, and it won't last. When a child obeys only out of fear of rejection, what happens when that fear stops? Treating children oppositely from the way God treats us can lead to relational strife and brokenness. If we want to see children learn to obey from a heart that desires the family's values, then they must be reminded of their identity time and time again. In their identity as part of the family, there is no fear of being kicked out. Instead, there is a constant assurance that they are not only part of the family but will grow to value what the family values over time.

Fear puts the fire under us. To live out the Christian life, and to adopt, we need the fire not under us but in us. Nothing lights up our heart for God and his kingdom like knowing that we are fully known and fully loved in Christ despite our sin.

FEELING HELPLESS

One time when our family was camping in the mountains and my kids were having fun splashing in the river, Anna decided to take our adopted daughter out into the river. Faith Ann was probably two at the time, and she couldn't walk. Suddenly, when Anna was in the exact middle of the river on a rock with Faith Ann, we heard a rushing of water. Over the course of about a minute, the spot where the kids were playing in ankle-deep water had become water about three feet high with a serious current. I took off into the river as fast as I could, and by the time I got to Anna, she was braced as best as she could be in waist-deep water, clinging to Faith Ann for dear life. Apparently, someone had opened a dam in anticipation of a storm. I had a hard time getting Anna and Faith Ann back to the bank safely. When I asked Anna if she was okay, her response was, "Yes, but I just felt so helpless."

Helplessness is a weighty feeling. If anyone embodied helplessness, it was Mephibosheth—an obscure character from the Old Testament. Imagine living three thousand years ago. Your family was once in power, but now your ancestors have all died. The new king, David, is the very man your grandfather Saul tried to kill. To make matters worse, you have no money, you're in hiding, and you were crippled in both feet at just five years old so that you can't walk. You have no rank at all. That's helpless.

In that day, the protocol was to eliminate everyone from the previous regime when a new one came to power.[3] Everyone would have expected David to kill any remaining members of Saul's family. But David did the opposite. He had made a promise to his friend Jonathan years earlier, and he intended to keep it. So David went looking for anyone from the house of Saul—not to punish them, but to bless them.

Think of it from Mephibosheth's perspective. The new king has come to power, and you know what that usually means—it's time to run. But you can't run, because you're lame in both feet. How helpless would that feel? Yet David doesn't bring judgment; he extends grace. He welcomes Mephibosheth into his household and treats him like one of his own sons. One commentator calls it a "stunning icon of divine grace."[4] Mephibosheth expected death. Instead, he received life, a position of prominence, and a permanent seat at the king's table.

Christians should deeply identify with Mephibosheth's story. In our sin, we were enemies of the rightful king, Jesus. We didn't deserve a place in his kingdom. In fact, our condition was even worse than that of Mephibosheth. He was lame in his limbs—we were lame in our souls. In sin, we couldn't walk back into God's kingdom even if we wanted to. Ephesians 2 describes us as spiritual orphans, cut off from the family of God. Choosing our own way placed us outside the household and made us strangers to the promises God gives his children. But because of Jesus's sacrifice, we could be brought back in—though someone had to carry us. Despite being spiritually lame, we have a greater King and a seat at an eternal table.

FEELING EMPOWERED TO ADOPT

When Christians reflect on what God has done for them, they naturally desire to extend that same grace to others. This was Mephibosheth's story—and it's ours, too. Later in his life, Mephibosheth would demonstrate great loyalty to the king. We can do the same when we are overwhelmed by the kindness God has shown us. Adoption is one of the clearest pictures of the gospel: We, who were not part of the original family, have been given a place at the table. We, who could not approach God on our own, were carried to him. That kind of grace stirs deep gratitude—a gratitude that compels us to reach out to others who find themselves on the outside, in need of someone to step in with compassion and love. Children awaiting adoption have much in common with Mephibosheth—they are on the periphery, hoping someone will see them and move toward them in grace.

In truth, we all spiritually resemble Mephibosheth, don't we? What God has done for us should inspire us to do the same for others. Who in your life needs a place in your family and at your table? Their story is not unlike our own. When we think of children in need of adoption, we should see ourselves in them. We should see our biological children in them. What God did for us provides the motivation for adoption. Next we will consider the meaning of adoption and see how that too pushes us to think about others.

REFLECTION QUESTIONS

- How are you being awakened to the difficulties of adoption and the need for a great motivation?
- How needy were you before God saved you through the gospel?
- What parallels do you see in your story and Mephibosheth's story (see 2 Samuel 9)?

4

The Meaning of Adoption

I chuckle when someone tells me they have "adopted" their dog. I understand that people love their pets and don't mean any comparison to children by saying this. After all, some people even dress their dogs in clothes! We live in a culture where the term *adoption* is often used loosely when referring to animals. So I bite my tongue and smile.

A similar thing happens every Christmas. At the local YMCA, or sometimes even in churches, there will be a ministry project for the needy. And sometimes people use adoption language around the ministry project.

But children aren't adopted for Christmas, and dogs aren't adopted at all. Not biblically speaking. Biblical adoption is legally bringing a person who is not part of your biological family into your family. In one example, a couple in our church adopted their second child, who was a biological sibling of the first child they had adopted. They are a living miracle of restoration—and now these children have a forever family.

Imprecise language can lead to misunderstanding—or stem from it. Either way, it's worthwhile to take a deeper look at the concept of adoption itself. Every person who becomes part of God's family does so through the spirit of adoption. Grasping the weight of the term *adoption* better positions us to stand in awe of God's grace. Jesus came so that we might become part of God's family through adoption. As adopted children, we gain full entrance into his family, we bear the family name, we have a relationship with God, and we have a future inheritance.

Recently, as a reluctant subscriber of Disney+, I saw Cinderella pop up, and it reminded me of the intense emotion I felt when I watched the movie as a kid. The Cinderella story is popular in our culture, but I don't think it's popular for the reason that we might assume. We tend to think it's beloved because Cinderella becomes a princess. However, I believe the real reason it resonates is because she isn't treated as a daughter. The tension created by the behavior of her stepmother and stepsisters is palpable. The story strikes a deep chord because of the favoritism lavished on the biological daughters. Even as children, we sense the injustice—and we feel the weight of the tragedy.

If you are a daughter in the family, you should expect the full rights and blessings of being part of that family. There shouldn't be favoritism toward one sibling over another because all the children share the same name. Intuitively, we understand something about adoption from a deep place in our hearts.

Let's articulate those feelings clearly and make sure they are firmly understood in our minds. Galatians 4 provides us with a deep dive into the inner workings of spiritual adoption:

> I mean that the heir, as long as he is a child, is no different from a slave, though he is the owner of everything, but he is under guardians and managers until the date set by his father. In the same way we also, when we were children, were enslaved to the elementary principles of the world. (vv. 1–3)

As he often does in Scripture, Paul uses an analogy that would have been easily understood at the time. Of course, in our day, it can feel a little fuzzy. In a wealthy household two thousand years ago, bondservants and children might have been running around together. Paul points out that when the children were young, an outsider may not have been able to identify which children were the actual sons of the household. But one day, as the children grew up, everything changed. That moment came when the father of the house bestowed the inheritance upon his son.

Before that day, the son would be under the authority of people he technically outranked because of his future status as the heir. In verse 3, Paul explains that this situation is similar to that of the children of God. Until the time set by the Father for them to fully step into their rights as sons, they are enslaved to the elementary principles of the world.

Admittedly, the term *elementary principles* is a bit complicated. In context, I believe it refers to the innate human tendency toward works-based righteousness. We naturally believe that we must earn our acceptance before God through our behavior. But then one day we hear the gospel and realize that becoming full sons of God comes not through striving, but by trusting in Jesus for our salvation. You could put it this way: People are held captive by their belief in works-based righteousness until they are set free by Jesus Christ. Across cultures and religions, people instinctively try to sacrifice to God or strive toward him through moral behavior—sometimes even through strange rituals and customs. I believe Paul's point is that even relying on God's law as a means of salvation is still a form of bondage to the elementary principles of the world. Regardless of the form it takes, trying to earn salvation apart from the gospel is doomed from the start.

In a marked moment, the children of God step into their full position as his sons and daughters. That moment occurs when we receive Christ and are declared part of God's family. As it is written, "But when the fullness of time had come, God sent forth his Son, born of woman, born under the law, to redeem those who were under the law, so that we might receive adoption as sons" (Galatians 4:4–5). In his wisdom, God sent Jesus Christ to redeem those under the law and to welcome them into his family through adoption. In doing so, he liberates us from the exhausting burden and enslavement of trying to earn our place through works.

I think it's worth pausing here. Not everyone reading this book has experienced that marked moment in their life. Have you? Are you still enslaved by the fear of not being good enough for God to accept you? Are you striving through works to become righteous before God? More to the point, is adoption a conversation your family is having for the wrong reason? Adopting for God's acceptance is no different from any other work we might try to perform. Are you living freely in the family of God, or are you still enslaved to the elementary principles of the world? If you are still enslaved, I would invite you to trust Jesus for salvation now. Admit you are a sinner, believe in Jesus's work, and confess him as the Lord of your life.

FROM SLAVES TO SONS

Becoming a Christian is a glorious event for many reasons—chief among them is full membership in the family of God. As members, we freely receive all the spiritual blessings that come from being part of his family.

Adoption means we are no longer slaves, but sons. We receive the family name, the relationship with our Father and spiritual siblings, and a magnificent future. Imagine the freedom and courage that come from knowing God has bestowed his very name upon us. The restored relationship with God is what we were created for. Through it, we gain not only the blessing of brothers and sisters in God's family but also a future to look forward to. What begins in this life continues into eternity. Christians aren't just made right with a judge; we are loved and cared for by God the Father.

Galatians 4:6 says, "And because you are sons, God has sent the Spirit of his Son into our hearts, crying, 'Abba! Father!'" God not only adopts us, but he also sends his Spirit to remind us, time and again, that we are his children. One of the haunting realities in some overseas orphanages is that the babies don't cry. The babies there learn very early that their cries go unheard and will not result in care. But that's not true for us as children of God. When we cry out to our Father, we know that he hears us, loves us, and cares for us.

Every year on March 7, Anna shows me a picture from the day we officially received Faith Ann's adoption decree. Although I'm pretty bad at remembering dates—birthdays and such—we love to celebrate not only the day Faith Ann was born but also the day she became a Hopper forever. On that day, she became fully part of our family. Our name became hers. Our culture became hers. All the love and care that a Hopper child receives from their parents became hers. And yes, a future inheritance became hers as well.

There are no Cinderellas in the family of God. Yet some of us struggle with this concept. Deep down, we may question whether God truly loves us and grants us such blessings. We might wonder, *Am I truly included despite my sin?* or, *Am I fully blessed despite my failures?* Until we resolve these questions, we cannot view adoption rightly.

Sometimes Christians view their relationship with God as if they need to perform well to secure a spot in his family. But that mindset makes it impossible to approach adoption from a healthy place. It's as if they are on our city's NBA G League team—the Greensboro Swarm. Swarm games are fun, and the talent is remarkable up close. G League players are usually on a ten-day contract and are often just one call away from moving up to the NBA. The pressure is intense—players have just ten days to prove they belong. If they perform well, they secure a spot; if not, they're out.

God doesn't bring us into his family just to see how we'll do. There are no ten-day contracts. How do we know that God accepts us despite our sin? Because he didn't bring us in based on our lack of sin in the first place. The gospel offers a better reality: God, for his own glory, moved toward us even in our sin. He bestows full adoption upon us and gives us the Spirit to assure us of his love. Knowing that we are secure for life frees us to grow in our faith without unhealthy fear. Adopted people are fully in the family—now and forever. Biblical adoption moves us from slaves to sons. Importantly, we also move toward others as God moved toward us.

FROM ADOPTED PEOPLE TO ADOPTING PEOPLE

When God adopts us as his children, we step fully into the family of God. There is no halfway, no "kind of" adoption. We live in a "kind of" culture—people "kind of" date and "kind of" commit their time. We often prefer to be only partially involved, always keeping an option for a way out. Thankfully, God doesn't approach adoption this way.

This is the greatest motivation we have for committing ourselves to adopt others. When we adopt a child, we are doing for them what God has done for us. In adoption, we bring others into our family fully—there is no halfway, no "kind of." We can extend this full commitment to others because it was done for us.

Some friends of ours met their now son, Eddie, while on a mission trip to Ecuador. Eddie, who has special needs, was abandoned as a newborn on the steps of an orphanage. Years after adopting Eddie, his parents learned more details about that day. Eddie had been found in a dumpster by a local carpenter who heard his cries. The carpenter pulled Eddie out and took him to the orphanage. He saved his life that day! Eddie's adopted father tells the story like this: "Eddie's story is my story as a Christian. I too was pulled from the dumpster and saved by a carpenter."

Christian, you are blessed, favored, forgiven, and loved. You are fully adopted. The inheritance is yours, and the family name is yours. You weren't created for an orphanage; you were created and called to be in the family of God. In the same way, children weren't created for orphanages; they were created for families.[1] God brought us into his family. Let us commit ourselves to the great pursuit of bringing orphans into ours.

REFLECTION QUESTIONS

- What has the term *adoption* meant to you, and how do you understand the term now?
- What blessings do you enjoy from being in the family of God?
- How do you see yourself in Eddie's story?

5

The Call to Adoption

Every Christian is called to use their specific giftings as they grow in their faith. Everything we do in life is intended to be leveraged for God's glory. This includes adopting. As we grow, adopting becomes an output of what God is doing in us spiritually. In this chapter, let's consider how we grow and how God can use us for his kingdom in general. Then we will apply that specifically to adoption.

The gospel shows us the love of God and gives us the desire to live for his mission. We want to live for the God who saves us. The gospel is like heat applied to metal. Without heat, metal can only be bent by force, and too much pressure can cause it to break. Also, once the pressure is removed, the metal often snaps back to its original form.[1] Religion can be like force—rules and fear may compel us to act for a time, but that kind of pressure doesn't lead to lasting transformation. We need to be softened, not just bent. We need to be pliable in the hands of God. We need the gospel that warms us so that God can shape us in a lasting, transformative way.

Chief among the changes God makes in our lives is our desire to serve him and his kingdom. *Sanctification* is a fancy theological word, but it simply means to become in practice what God declares us to be in truth. Because of the gospel, God sees us through the lens of the perfection of his Son, Jesus Christ. As we grow in our faith, our actual lives begin to align in practical ways with God's vision for us. A key part of that process is our growing desire for what God desires.

I'll never forget playing on the basketball team as a high school freshman. My dad wasn't a basketball player; in fact, he often poked fun at the game by calling it "roundball." I'm sure he was excited about me playing, but he didn't have much coaching to offer when it came to basketball. However, that all changed one day after a game when I got in the car to ride home.

I could tell something was off. Kids learn to read the room, and I picked up on the fact that my dad wasn't happy. I wasn't exactly sure what was wrong, but I had a sneaking suspicion it had to do with my lack of effort during the game. I had been influenced by some varsity guys who played with a lackadaisical style. They were skilled, but they weren't known for hustling back on defense or diving for loose balls.

I was probably fifteen at the time, caught in an awkward moment where I didn't know what was about to happen. Was I about to get a talking to, or had I engaged in some kind of "spankable" offense? The ride home was quiet and uncomfortable until my dad finally broke the silence with a single sentence: "You are my son, and in this family, you will hustle, or you will not play." That was it, but it was more than enough. He wasn't suggesting that my lack of hustle put my status in the family at risk—that would be bending the metal with rules and fear. Rather, he was focusing on my identity as a Hopper, reminding me of something fundamental: Hoppers hustle. That was a reality tied to my identity. In the game, I wasn't acting in line with who I was. The silent ride, and the subsequent speech, called me back to truth.

Although I didn't become a great basketball player, from that day forward I put one hundred percent effort into my play. I did so because that's what we, as Hoppers, do.

Christian sanctification is much like this. Throughout our lives, God continually reminds us of our new identity as members of his family. As we remember and embrace our place in the family, we act more and more like family members. Our actions begin to reflect who we truly are. A key aspect of this growth is living more and more for God's glory and mission. It's crucial to consider the broader life God calls us to live. Christians often do things that are different from what the world values and for different reasons. We've been brought into God's family to use everything he's given us for his mission on earth. But what does being on mission actually look like? The apostle Paul uses another metaphor to help us understand this. He says we are part of the body of Christ.

PART OF THE BODY

Romans 12 is extremely helpful in moving Christians from a life of selfishness to a life of selflessness. God saves us and gifts us to be used for his mission. Jesus didn't die on the cross to create spectators; he died to create servants for his mission. The gospel creates workers, not watchers.

Paul writes,

> For as in one body we have many members, and the members do not all have the same function, so we, though many, are one body in Christ, and individually members one of another. Having gifts that differ according to the grace given to us, let us use them. (Romans 12:4–6)

Here, "members" refers to body parts, and the idea is both simple and profound: A unified body is created by the diversity of its parts, each contributing to the movement and function of the whole body. The gist of this passage is that God's people form a singular body that is used for his mission, with every believer playing a vital role. We are not an audience watching the work of a few talented individuals; rather, we are like an army moving together to accomplish the mission.

Think of it like a car—a single machine composed of many parts. In fact, most cars have around thirty thousand individual components! A car is not the same thing as its parts. It is not merely a bumper, a starter, or a spark plug, but rather a functional entity made up of all these components coming together.

Our spiritual gifts, talents, wirings, and blessings all contribute to how we uniquely help the body of Christ function. Each of us was created with a purpose, a destiny, and a calling. God equips us in diverse ways throughout our lives to help the body of Christ fulfill its purpose. This isn't a vague notion; it's very specific. In Ephesians Paul explains, "For we are his workmanship, created in Christ Jesus for good works, which God prepared beforehand, that we should walk in them" (2:10). My friend and mentor J. D. Greear once said, "We only get one shot to go around this life. I want to make the biggest splash for the kingdom that I can!" This sentiment resonated deeply in my soul, and I hope it does for you as well.

The point is that we are the product of God's work within us. We are his workmanship, created and recreated through the gospel by Jesus to do the good works he prepared for us beforehand! We are not all the same body part. If every part was the same, we wouldn't be a body; we would be a monstrosity. The diversity of our gifts, talents, and experiences brings about the richness and functionality of the body.

A UNIQUE BODY PART

If you're part of the body, then you're a specific body part. Think back to the car analogy: If something isn't working and I walked into an auto shop, I wouldn't just ask for "a car part." The attendant would immediately reply, "Which one?" If I said, "I don't know—just a part," we wouldn't get anywhere. Every part of a car has a unique purpose and part number, just like every part of the body has a distinct function. The same is true in the body of Christ. If you belong to the body, you are a body part. So which part are you? The answer has everything to do with how God has gifted you for his purposes.

Consider this illustration. On June 9, 1973, at the Belmont Stakes, the racehorse Secretariat lined up with a chance to become the first winner of the Triple Crown in twenty-five years.[2] But no one could believe what was happening halfway through the race—Secretariat was gaining speed at every pole. In fact, many worried the horse would push too hard and be unable to sustain the pace. The Belmont Stakes is a long race, and some feared that Secretariat might exhaust himself—or even run himself to death—driving to maintain such a blistering speed.

On that day, Secretariat did the unthinkable. Instead of fading, he picked up speed throughout the race. Coming into the last stretch, Secretariat grew even stronger. He surged forward with a powerful last kick and won the race by an astounding thirty-one lengths. Announcer Chic Anderson made the now-famous call: "Secretariat is widening now. He is moving like a tremendous machine."[3] To everyone's amazement, the horse ran a mile and a half in two minutes and twenty-four seconds flat—a record that stands to this day.

How could Secretariat move like that? When he died years later, veterinarians examined his body and discovered something remarkable: The average thoroughbred's heart weighs about nine pounds, but Secretariat's heart weighed twenty-two pounds! The doctors noted that it wasn't pathologically enlarged; it was just naturally huge. This allowed him to pump more blood and cycle oxygen more efficiently. In other words, Secretariat was built to run.

Christians are the same way. God has gifted you in some area with a proverbial heart twice the size of others. In that area, you will excel in ministry because of your unique gifts and talents. Unfortunately, too many Christians live as "generic" body parts. They come to church and do the dance, but they lack passion for God's mission because they never personally and specifically connect to it.

We feel out of place when we generically connect to the mission without tapping into the specific area where we're gifted. But we feel the electricity of God's mission when his works and our giftings align. I've met truly "on fire" believers, and I've met very bored believers. Often, the difference is simply whether they've found a ministry that matches and utilizes their God-given gifts. Are you connected to what you were created for?

The fact that you are reading this book shows that you have some passion for and inclination toward adoption. If God is giving you both the passion and the opportunity, he has likely shaped you for it. There is a reason that you get excited when you hear adoption stories. There is a reason that God continues to give you opportunities and a community where this topic keeps coming up. It may very well be that he wired you, gifted you, and is guiding you toward an adoption calling that he created you for. Whatever passions and giftings God has given us, using them isn't optional; it's essential if we want to make our greatest impact for the kingdom of God.

DIFFERING GIFTS

"Having gifts that differ according to the grace given to us, let us use them" (Romans 12:6). God gifts us both naturally and supernaturally for the works he calls us to. As we all have gifts according to his grace, are we using them in the real world? Some people may hide behind the excuse of not knowing exactly how they are gifted. However, it's not just about *understanding* our gifts, but about a *commitment to use them* in God's service. Will we use our gifts to glorify him?

I do not believe this passage refers only to the supernatural spiritual gifts. We are all wired in different ways, and we each have unique experiences and talents. The Bible does tell us that we are gifted supernaturally by God, but that also means that we are built to run hard for his kingdom in specific ways.

We are all called to steward the gifts God gives us. For some, this might look like excelling in business to financially contribute to kingdom causes. For others, it could mean preaching the gospel, or saying yes to God's international mission by becoming a missionary. For some, it might involve full devotion to homeschooling your kids and seeing them grow in Christian maturity. There are as many applications of the charge to "use your gifts" as there are people reading this book.

For some, applying this passage might mean adopting a child (or children) and raising them in the faith. Maybe it is time to pause and ask whether adoption is something you should do. Not everyone is called to adopt, but more people than are adopting should consider it. Do you have a home? Does your heart break for the outsider? Can you financially support a child coming into your home? Do you have a church family who will stand behind you and hold the rope? When you hear adoption stories, does your heart burn in your chest? If you find yourself answering "yes" to some of these questions, then maybe God has prepared an adoption beforehand that you should walk in. Maybe we should ask, Are we gifted to walk in adoption?

Jesus died to create servants, not spectators. He is calling us from the sidelines to the front lines in some area. You are a piece of the puzzle. You are a body part. There is no such thing as an uncalled or ungifted Christian. And just as you can't be a Navy SEAL without seeing combat or a ballplayer without taking swings, you can't be a thriving Christian without using your God-given gifts for the mission. If you are gifted for adoption, then step forward and embrace that calling. As we will see in the next chapter, saying yes to adoption can be very fruitful for the mission of God.

REFLECTION QUESTIONS

- How is your individual spiritual growth fueled by dwelling on the gospel?
- In what ways do your God-given gifts align with the call to adoption?
- How are you wrestling with the financial question of whether you should adopt?

6

The Mission of Adoption

One family in our church adopted from a country in South America. They prepared to bring their child home by learning Spanish, making travel plans, and getting their house ready. When the time came, they traveled to meet their child and bring her home. These folks were on a mission! But it wasn't actually a mission for adoption. It was a mission for the glory of God.

The larger mission of living for God's glory played out for them in adoption. In this chapter, I want to show how adoption is part of the larger mission of every Christian. First, let's think about mission, and then we can look at ways that adoption fits into that mission.

A MISSION FOCUSES OUR LIFE

Each of us is on a mission. Some are driven to make money, others to build a reputation, and others to marry and start a family. Regardless of our personal missions, God has a greater mission for each and every one of us. His mission is for us to use our lives to bring him glory. This can manifest in many ways, but one of the most crucial is making disciples. A significant part of glorifying God is proclaiming his glory to the world.

Is that a mission you're on? I have many missions in my life. I am a husband and a father. I'm a hobby farmer. I'm a coach and an athlete (though I'm not claiming to be a very good one!). I have goals I want to accomplish in many areas of my life. I'm goal-oriented, and having a bigger mission as a believer doesn't squash or overshadow the other goals—it simply reframes them. It puts them in proper perspective. It clarifies some and pushes others out if they don't align with the big picture.

One way to think about the glory of God is to imagine the weight of one thing displacing something lighter. In fact, the very word *glory* can be understood in terms of weight and significance. I took my oldest daughter to a family camp in Northern California, and we would agree it was one of the best weeks of our lives. We tackled tons of adventurous activities, made new friends, and had plenty of one-on-one time to connect. On the first day, the camp hosted a lake day, which was a blast. There was a slide, an extremely high rope swing, and, you guessed it, a blob.

If you haven't seen a blob before, it's essentially a giant inflatable air pillow floating in the water. When used correctly, it can launch someone fifteen feet into the air—or more! The setup involves one person lying on one end—we'll call them the *blobbee*. Another person (or two) jumps off a platform—these are the *blobbers*. When the blobbers land on their end of the pillow, they send the blobbee soaring into the air and into the water.

It was incredibly fun watching everyone take their turn on the blob, and eventually my daughter convinced me to give it a try. She even persuaded two large men to make me the blobbee. As I looked up from the blob and saw them preparing to jump in unison, I remember thinking, *That's 600 pounds of man coming down on this thing! What's going to happen?* Well, I went flying.

The blob is a simple illustration of what happens when the glory of God becomes a central desire in our lives. When God's glory comes into focus, it carries such weight that it displaces lesser things. If our missions are centered on ourselves—our money, our name, our marriage, or something else—God's glory will either reframe or completely displace those smaller missions. Some pursuits get bounced if they don't align with God's glory, while others are reshaped so they can be used for his glory. The point is, growing Christians see the mission of their lives as bringing glory to God by sharing him with others.

ADOPTION PROVIDES AN OPEN DOOR

If we are living for God's mission, then we must consider the evangelistic power of adoption. Adoption isn't just motivated by the gospel—it is also a powerful testimony for the gospel. As I've stated, outside of marriage, adoption is perhaps the clearest picture we have of the gospel. When we step into the waters of adoption, we raise questions from the watching world. Why would you adopt if you're able to have biological children? That question gives us a chance to share the gospel. After all, for us, adoption is more about theology than biology.[1]

Colossians 4 instructs us to walk in a way that raises questions about our new lives in Christ. Paul asks for prayers that God would "open a door" for the gospel. Sometimes God opens a door for us to share when people are intrigued about our Christian lives. Their intrigue leads to questions, and those questions are open doors for us to share the reason for the hope within us.

The normal Christian life is a radical life by the world's standards. It's a question-raising, head-scratching life. Why put others before yourself, give away your money, invest your time in others, or adopt and foster children? Who would choose to live this way? But when Christians embrace and live the radically normal life, others take notice. The world's questions are our open doors.

While adoption is a significant part of this, it's not the whole picture. This conversation stretches back to the earliest days of our faith and touches many areas of life today. Early Christians raised eyebrows because they refused to share their wives yet freely shared their money—completely opposite of the Roman cultural ethos. They also cared for the poor, prompting Emperor Julian to famously lament, "The godless Galileans care not only for their own poor but for ours as well."[2] From the beginning, Christians have lived in ways that are difficult to understand from the outside.

The same is true today. Imagine being in a competitive work environment where everyone is trying to outdo others, even outside of work. During the summer, the office buzzes with tales of extravagant vacations, each one trying to top the last. Picture one man saying, "Our vacation this summer was over the top—white sandy beaches in the Caribbean, a Jet Ski, and an open bar. I really upped the game! We even brought a nanny so that we didn't have to worry about the kids. It was epic!"

Now imagine him turning to a radically normal Christian and asking about his vacation. Standing by the watercooler, the Christian responds, "Man, our trip was unbelievable! I took my oldest daughter, and we rode unair-conditioned trains through the wilds of India. We slept in block buildings without electricity or plumbing and were sick and exhausted for most of the trip. But, look at this picture! This is a pastor we met in a remote village where he's seeing the Lord move in the hearts of an unreached people. We prayed for him and had the opportunity to share resources from our church. The trip changed my life!"

At this point, all the non-Christians around the watercooler are probably thinking, *This dude is weird!* But I bet they're also asking, *Why would anyone choose to spend their limited vacation time and money this way? What drives someone to invest so much in a trip like that?* An intrigued world asks questions about why we live this way—and that, my friends, is a wide-open door.

The door to evangelism flies wide open when we walk in adoption. I know this firsthand because I've seen "the look." The open door has a look, and it's the look a non-Christian gives when they're intrigued by your life but don't quite know how to ask why you live the way you do. People are fascinated by adoption—they think it's admirable. Yet they often don't understand why anyone would choose it unless they have no other option to build a family. Even then, I'm not sure the modern generation fully grasps it.

At some point, I promise, the curiosity about your decision to adopt will be too much for some folks to ignore. They'll come to you with that unmistakable "open-door look" and ask, "Why did you choose to adopt?" And praise God that we have a life-giving answer: We adopted because God adopted us.

We recently saw someone come to faith and get baptized at our church, and my heart was truly warmed when I heard his story. One of the reasons he chose to follow Jesus was because of the example set by his boss—an ordinary believer from our congregation whose life looked radically different from the outside.

What stood out was how he treated his family, how much he loved the church, and how he lived on mission. He was also a "Rope Holder." At our church, we have a Rope Holder ministry specifically designed to support families who are adopting or fostering by serving them in practical ways.

For the new believer in my story, the fact that his boss was a Rope Holder just baffled him. Why would anyone take the time, pain, and responsibility to care so deeply for people who weren't even blood relatives? What would drive someone to live this way? This question was one of many open doors that ultimately led to his salvation.

If being a Rope Holder can raise that type of question, adoption can also raise questions. In fact, countless aspects of adoption raise questions. Isn't it expensive? Absolutely, but not compared to the price God paid for me to be in his family. Isn't it hard on your other kids at times? More than you could possibly know. But hard doesn't mean bad. God uses brothers and sisters in our families and church families to build us into who he is calling us to be. Every part of an adoption journey connects to the gospel and can be used for God's mission. That mission is good to keep in mind as we move to the next chapter because adoption always involves deep joy and high cost.

REFLECTION QUESTIONS

- How would someone looking in from the outside describe the mission you're living for?
- How does the weight of God's glory push out smaller "missions" you may be living for?
- In what ways do you see adoption as an open door to share the gospel?

7

The Cost and Joy of Adoption

A family in our church adopted a child with severe special needs. Now everything in their life revolves around caring for her. Her needs have radically impacted their finances and relationships. Adoption is a costly endeavor. When Jesus calls us into his family, he tells us to count the cost. We must give up many things to enter the kingdom of God. Jesus also said that if we are to follow him, we must take up our cross (Luke 9:23–24). Following Jesus is hard, but it's absolutely worth it. Adoption is much the same. It is financially, relationally, and spiritually costly—but it is worth it.

COSTLY OBEDIENCE

You are likely aware that adoption is expensive. I recently met with the head of a prominent adoption agency who informed me that the current cost of adoption ranges between $20,000 and $35,000. While there are tax refunds and numerous programs to assist with these expenses, every adoption story I know involves significant financial commitment from the adoptive family and their church community.

The cost of adoption is a legitimate barrier to entry. While many people might be able to handle an expense of tens of thousands of dollars at some point in their lives, that time is often not during their mid-twenties to mid-thirties—the prime years when many consider adopting. The conversation about funding an adoption can be daunting. In my opinion, the financial requirement is likely one main reason that many Christian families hesitate to consider adoption. Perhaps they don't have the funds readily available, or they are simply uncomfortable with the idea of asking others for financial support.

God often uses uncomfortable situations to grow our faith. It is true that adoption will cost us dearly. How does that speak to the value God placed upon us by bearing the cost of our adoption? The money we spend to adopt a child should heighten our sense to the price God paid to adopt us.

There was a cost for every Christian chosen, or adopted, into the family of God. The price of this adoption was far higher than any monetary amount. It cost God the life of his Son, Jesus Christ, to bring us back into his family. One way the Bible describes salvation is the settling of a debt (Colossians 2:13–14). In our sin, we incurred a debt that we could never repay. Our future was destined to be eternally separate from God because of this debt. But God gladly paid the cost to bring us into the family. If someone asks, "How much does adoption cost?" our response can be, "Not nearly as much as it cost God to adopt me."

Although it may feel counterintuitive at first, there's great joy in inviting others to join you in funding an adoption. When

Anna and I were in the process of adopting Faith Ann, we did just that. While we didn't make a broad public appeal, we intentionally invited our family to be part of the journey. It was important to me to ask them to give because I wanted them to buy into the vision of our family's changing landscape. They helped us tremendously, and we are truly and eternally grateful. If I hadn't invited them in, I would have robbed them of a tremendous blessing. Faith Ann is a bright spot in our lives, and her story has already impacted so many people. Anyone who contributed to her adoption likely grew in their relationship with the Lord and experienced deeper joy. What a blessing!

Travel is another significant cost. While not every adoption requires extensive travel, all adoptions involve some degree of it. For international adoptions, the travel burden is often much heavier—ranging from a couple of weeks to several months and sometimes involving multiple trips. Travel is one of the many sacrifices that adoptive parents make for the mission.

One family in our church experienced this firsthand. Due to complications with paperwork, they made the difficult decision for one parent to live overseas until the issues were resolved. The family was separated for months. It was an incredibly trying time—the cost and stress were high—but travel was simply part of the process.

When people travel to adopt a child, they are literally going to bring their child home. Someone is willingly disrupting their life for weeks or even months in order to bring a child into their family. Isn't there joy in seeing that as a powerful picture of what God has done for us? We could never get to God on our own. For us to become part of his family, Jesus came for us. Jesus traveled. God sent forth his Son. Just like a child who cannot come to their new family on their own, we couldn't come to God—so he came for us (Galatians 4:4–5).

LOVE THAT STRETCHES THE FAMILY

Another issue that brings both cost and joy is the effect that adoption has on siblings. In many adoptions, parents welcome a child, while siblings also gain a new brother or sister. For adoptive families, this brings deep joy. I love the feature on our phones that pulls up old pictures and creates collages from years past. Recently, one of these collages popped up from the week we brought Faith Ann home from the hospital. I don't think I've ever seen my kids smile so widely. They were thrilled to welcome a new member of the family. When Faith Ann came home, sibling bonds began to form—bonds that will last throughout their lives.

Deep sibling bonds are joyful, but as with anything in life, there is no joy without sacrifice. Our kids' lives have been deeply enriched by Faith Ann, but that doesn't mean they haven't made significant sacrifices. In fact, they've given up a lot. Our family's life looks different from most. No matter what we're doing, there's always a component that changes things. Faith Ann has Down syndrome and is nonverbal. She moves at a slower pace and often doesn't fully understand what's happening around her. This means we can't simply pick up and go. Every activity requires careful planning. For example, attending the kids' ball games isn't as simple as just loading up and heading out. Our plans often involve arranging for a babysitter, or taking two cars so that someone can leave early when Faith Ann needs to go home.

In addition, Faith Ann's greater needs requiring Anna's time have sometimes meant the other kids receive less attention. God has been gracious to us, and this full-time dependency is improving as Faith Ann grows. However, for years, our kids didn't experience having both parents present at their events. At home or at church, they often had to manage things on their own in ways that other children their ages might not have had to. Oftentimes, dinner at our house doesn't include both Anna and me digging into our kids' days to discover their highs and lows. Instead, it typically means one parent—and you can guess which one—attending to Faith Ann to ensure that she is fed and cared for.

Our kids also must cope with emotional issues that other families may not face. For most families, a baby getting a cold doesn't usually result in a trip to the doctor or the hospital. But that was our reality for years. We've had emergency services visit our house many times for issues related to Faith Ann's special needs.

One Sunday morning when Faith Ann was young, our eight-year-old daughter, HattieJo, was tasked with getting her up to be fed and clothed for church. As HattieJo prepared Faith Ann, she discovered that Faith Ann's G-tube had come out. When a G-tube comes out, it needs to be replaced immediately or will require surgical reinsertion. I was already at church that morning, so HattieJo had to hold Faith Ann's arms while Anna struggled to get it back in. Despite Faith Ann's cries, they did get the G-tube back in—praise God! I didn't think much about it at the time because it was just our reality, but looking back, I question how an event like this affects an eight-year-old girl.

To be clear, for myself, Anna, and our other children, Faith Ann is the greatest blessing God has ever given us. When we do our "thankful tree" every Thanksgiving, Faith Ann is always at the top of the list, no matter whose turn it is to choose. We love her, have so much fun because of her, and can't believe that God handpicked us to be her family. I know our children will be deeper people because they have Faith Ann as a sister. However, there is no denying that it is hard on our children as well as us. It's deeply joyful and deeply costly.

SPIRITUAL WARFARE

Adoption is spiritual warfare, and warfare is costly. When Christian adoptive parents bring a child home, they are diving headlong into a spiritual battle. It may sound harsh, but it's their reality. Satan hates children and thrives on family breakdown. How many times in Scripture do we see leaders ordering the genocide of children? From the earliest pages of Scripture, we know the eventual serpent-crushing Savior would be born as a baby into this world. Satan had no problem attempting to snuff out this line through mass genocide.

Statistically, most people become Christians after being raised in Christian homes. Considering this reality, the quickest way for Satan to disrupt the transfer of Christianity from one generation to the next is by breaking up families. So if displacing children by breaking up homes is Satan's desire, then Christian adoption must be sickening to him. Christian adoption is not a peripheral issue in the spiritual battle—it is at the center. As Christians step deeper into adoption, the kingdom of darkness won't take it lying down.

Throughout Scripture, we see the reality of spiritual warfare clearly depicted. Ephesians 6 provides a powerful example:

> Finally, be strong in the Lord and in the strength of his might. Put on the whole armor of God, that you may be

> able to stand against the schemes of the devil. For we do not wrestle against flesh and blood, but against the rulers, against the authorities, against the cosmic powers over this present darkness, against the spiritual forces of evil in the heavenly places. (vv. 10–12)

This text unmistakably shows that God is preparing his children for a spiritual fight that Satan wants to bring to their doorstep. And bring the fight Satan does!

Satan typically operates in both everyday life and the supernatural realm. Scripture provides abundant examples of Satan operating in everyday life. For instance, the root of much false teaching is ordinary demonic activity. Paul writes in 1 Timothy 4:1, "Now the Spirit expressly says that in later times some will depart from the faith by devoting themselves to deceitful spirits and teachings of demons." In these environments, people aren't speaking in strange voices, and they don't resemble a horror movie, but demonic influence and spiritual warfare are still present. Similarly, when we believe or spread lies, we engage in spiritual warfare. Jesus tells us in John 8:44 that Satan is a liar by his very nature. Paul echoes this concern in 2 Corinthians 11:3, expressing his fear that the church might be led astray by Satan's cunning, just as Eve was.

Many of us believe lies about ourselves and others. While some of these thoughts may stem from our flesh, a significant portion are rooted in spiritual warfare. We often hold beliefs about ourselves that we would never offer to someone else as advice. For example, many people quietly believe that abuse they suffered was their own fault. This is a powerful example of the ordinary demonic at work.

On the other hand, sometimes spiritual warfare breaks out in supernatural ways. Scripture gives examples of Satan attempting to capture people's attention with fear and amazement, including in the stories of the maniac of Gadara (Matthew 8) and the sons of Sceva (Acts 19). In another instance, the Bible tells us in Matthew 12:22 that Jesus healed a blind and mute man by casting out a demon that was causing his condition.

Why the quick survey of spiritual warfare? It's simple: Many Christians assume spiritual warfare is something they'll never encounter. They believe it only happens in missionary settings deep in the jungle. In reality, we often don't see it because we're not expecting the fight to come to our doorstep. When it does, we chalk it up to ordinary occurrences. The truth is that Satan leans in when we lean in. Where the mission is advancing, spiritual warfare intensifies—and adoption is one of the hottest parts of the battle.

Spiritual warfare is tricky. When families step into adoption, it's possible that the enemy may respond with supernatural attacks—sickness, relational disruption, mental health struggles, and more. Is it scary? Yes. But it's also part of the cost of doing battle.

In all of this, we must remember that in Christ, we are more than conquerors (Romans 8:37). No one wants to have to endure the attacks of Satan, but there is great joy in knowing we have final victory in Christ. The one who holds our future also calls us not to fear, because he is with us. When God supernaturally brings us through an adoption roadblock, we rejoice.

I cannot tell you how many times attacks of the enemy were met with intercessory prayer and faith as our friends stepped in on our behalf. What a joy it is to have brothers and sisters in the trenches with you! In fact, that joy will be the focus of our next chapter. Adoption is not a solo mission. Adoptive families will need support as they endure the joys and costs of this calling.

REFLECTION QUESTIONS

- If you're honest, are finances the biggest barrier keeping you from saying yes to adoption?
- Although adoption will cost the other children in your home something, have you considered the immense joy it could bring them?
- What fears do you have about the spiritual warfare that often comes with adoption?

8

The Community of Adoption

Christian adoption is a team game. I know of one family in our church who expressed how their community was integral to their adoption process. Because they were adopting through the foster system, there were endless meetings, and finding childcare for their other children was always a challenge. It was a grind. Without the support of their Christian community, it would have been much harder. When families step into adoption, the support of other families is primarily needed in three areas: finance, prayer, and practical living.

I know this firsthand. Our Christian community stepped up before Faith Ann even came home. These individuals were investors in her story—our family, friends, and a few people who specifically sought me out to help. Toward the end of the funding process, one brother invited me to lunch and got right to the point, asking, "How much is left to fund the adoption?" Within twenty-four hours, the exact sum was in our funding account due to his family's generosity. They loved us well and put that love into action. We received their generosity as a gift from God, and we are still grateful to this day.

Faith Ann was in the hospital for the first couple of months after she was born. During that difficult time, our community group and other friends really stepped up. They brought us meals and offered to watch our other kids on days when we both needed to travel. They constantly asked for updates so they could pray specifically and boldly on Faith Ann's behalf.

Then I got the flu, and the hospital wouldn't allow anyone from our home to visit Faith Ann. Our sweet girl was in a hospital almost two hours away, and up until that point, one of us was there to hold her and pray with her every day. When some friends from another church in the same city as the hospital heard about our plight, they stepped in. They told us not to worry, and they went to the hospital to hold her and pray. I'm not sure where we would be today without these people in our life.

In the last chapter, I mentioned that financing adoption is a significant issue. Adoption costs a lot of money, and that is an obstacle for many. It shouldn't be. Fundraising for adoption is a double win. Asking our Christian community to support adoption isn't just beneficial for the adoptive child and family, but it's also a tremendous spiritual opportunity for givers. Yes, you read that right—it's not only a good thing for those directly involved in the adoption, but it's an incredible opportunity for spiritual growth among the donors as well. In the economy of God's kingdom, whatever takes the ministry the farthest also takes the disciple the deepest. Giving doesn't just fund the ministry; it is a God-ordained discipline that helps believers dethrone the idol of money and grow in their faith.

Some people may hesitate to share their need for adoption funds with their community for fear of coming off like a slick used car salesman. But asking someone to partner in a kingdom cause, with the understanding that their commitment will help them grow, changes the entire conversation. Suddenly, they are no longer just a cog in the wheel to help you achieve your goals; instead, they become a beloved family member or friend who you invite into a deeper relationship with the Lord through the opportunity of your adoption. This change in perspective makes all the difference. Shifting from feeling like a slick used car salesman to becoming a true kingdom partner happens after we grasp the key truth that giving is not just a *fruit* of maturity, but also a *pathway to* maturity.

GIVING: TRAVELING A PATHWAY TO MATURITY

Too often we think of generosity solely as a sign of spiritual growth, and that is to our detriment. It limits our understanding. Is generosity a fruit of Christian maturity? Absolutely! As people grow in their faith, they naturally want to give more of themselves. After all, Jesus didn't offer just a portion of his blood—he gave it all. There's no doubt that generosity is a fruit of maturity. But we shouldn't wait to call people to generosity until they're "mature enough" to handle it. Instead, generosity should be one of the first things we discuss with new Christians.

Take the story of the rich young ruler for example (Mark 10:17–22). While the young man seemingly obeyed all the commandments, Jesus cut to the heart of his immaturity by telling him to give his money away. For the rich young ruler, this wasn't a fruit of maturity; it was the pathway to it.

In Matthew 6:21, Jesus says, "Where your treasure is, there your heart will be also." When you give toward something, your heart gets wrapped up in it! Financial outputs come from spiritual inputs, but it's also true that spiritual outputs come from financial inputs. Colossians 1 tells us that God is before all things. He is first in our lives. When this truth resides in our hearts, we tend to give more freely. And as we give more, we increasingly cherish that truth in our lives.

What does this have to do with inviting others to join us in funding adoption? In short, everything! When we ask someone to give toward a Christian adoption, we are not just using them to fund our ministry or family. Instead, we are giving them an opportunity to grow in their relationship with God by tying their heart to what he loves through giving. God calls taking care of orphans pure religion (James 1:27), and giving helps us to love what God loves. That is more than an invitation for someone to help you. You are inviting them into an opportunity to grow.

What is your heart posture toward those you would ask to help fund your adoption? You are providing them a tremendous opportunity to grow, but do you see it that way? Are they in your path to help you do "your thing," or would God have you ask them so he can grow them? Where you land on that thirty-thousand-foot question changes everything. I have not discussed grants, tax credits, and fundraising events because those things only come into play after a more central idea. Jesus didn't die to create spectators. God calls people to walk in specific works for him and for their growth. For so many people, giving to an adoption is one of those works. Let's not rob people of that opportunity. I've literally never seen an unfunded adoption, but I know some people never start for fear of that happening. Don't live in fear! Flip the mindset, give people an opportunity to grow, and see what God will do!

SUPPORTING: HOLDING THE ROPE

Beyond finances, adoptive families need others to come alongside them to support them in prayer and practice. They need others to "hold the rope." William Carey embarked for India to share the gospel there in 1793, a significant milestone at that time. Today, we have mission boards and celebrations in Christian circles around sending people to other nations, but that wasn't the norm in the late eighteenth century. Carey and his associates had to build a culture of sending, and a major part of that culture involved supporting missionaries on the field. While going may seem like the more glamorous part, the support from home is just as crucial.

Carey had a famous one-liner for his friend Andrew Fuller as they discussed his impending departure for India: "I will go down into the pit if you will hold the rope."[1] What a powerful image of support! Carey was essentially saying that he would venture into the darkness of an unreached land, a region gripped by Satan for thousands of years, to bring the light of the gospel. He was willing to descend into this spiritual pit, trusting that Fuller would support him and not let him fall.

Fuller answered Carey's call. While William Carey is known and celebrated as the father of modern missions, he wouldn't have been able to fulfill his mission without Andrew Fuller and others like him. Fuller established mission boards, raised funds, spoke passionately about missions, and kept people informed about the work in India. In short, he held the rope.

By God's grace, we have cultivated a strong sending culture at Mercy Hill Church, where I serve as lead pastor, and we strive to support missionaries as faithfully and effectively as possible. For us, this means ensuring that our missionaries have support teams regularly checking on them and praying for them. We mobilize prayer groups and make a concerted effort to send teams primarily to spend time with our people on the field. As Fuller did for Carey, we aim to hold the rope for our sent ones.

In addition, we've embraced the concept and language of holding the rope when it comes to adoption and foster care. We have ambitious goals of raising people up to build families in the way God builds his. We understand that our ministry, Chosen, will only be as strong as those who commit to it. Those walking the difficult road of adoption need others in their corner to offer encouragement and tangible support. Every adoptive and foster care family needs someone to hold the rope.

During Christian adoption, families often find themselves like those dangling at the end of a rope, deep in a pit. In this state, they are fully dependent on others to hold that rope securely for them. Satan will target these families with everything he has to disrupt the mission—sickness, financial strain, relational conflict, loss, issues with social services, and other obstacles. He will throw everything at them. The church must respond by throwing everything it has in their support!

At Mercy Hill, we have learned how to grow practically in supporting adoptive and foster families. Initially, we focused on connecting adoptive families to a community group, assuming the group would naturally provide the care they needed. And while our groups are amazing at serving, encouraging, and praying for these families, we soon realized that casting a big vision for adoption required a more specialized approach. So we developed an official volunteer role called the Rope Holder. What does a Rope Holder do? In short, they do what's needed. Some Rope Holders primarily give financial support, while others help with childcare or offer consistent prayer. Some are skilled at organizing events. Regardless of their specific role, all Rope Holders are committed to supporting families who are on the front lines.

Adoptive families need three primary things. First, they need prayer and encouragement. If Satan is going to bring the fight, we need to be on our knees. Prayer isn't just preparation for the battle; it is the battle itself. John Piper famously described prayer as a wartime walkie-talkie.[2] Prayer moves the hand that moves the world, so we need Rope Holders who are committed to praying for the adoptive families in our churches.

The power of prayer was evident in our story. Our church collectively held the rope in praying for Faith Ann's heart as we waited for her to grow enough to undergo open-heart surgery. Our church asked God to miraculously heal her, which he did! At a year in, while the doctors were still awaiting her growth, other tissue grew around the hole in her heart and compensated for the defect. By the time Faith Ann was three and a half, she was released from cardiology with no restrictions and no surgery—praise God! It was an absolute miracle that God used to build my faith. I believe this was nothing short of an answer to the prayers of our church members as they held the rope for us.

These families on the front lines also need encouragement along what can be a long, arduous journey. Our own adoption process took fourteen months from start to placement, and it wasn't finalized for another year or so after that. We've known families whose journeys took double or even triple that amount of time. There's plenty of room for discouragement along the way. That's where Rope Holders can lift these families up when they're down or the road feels long.

Second, adoptive families need financial support. As Randy Alcorn famously said of all our possessions: "You can't take it with you—but you *can* send it on ahead."[3] Jesus makes this clear in Matthew 6:19: "Do not lay up for yourselves treasures on earth." We are called to invest in God's kingdom by using our resources for things of eternal significance.

In 2020, our church made a corporate commitment to financially support adoptive parents. Just before the world shut down due to COVID-19, I concluded a sermon series focused specifically on adoption. As part of that series, we challenged the congregation to give generously so that we, as the local church, could be the first partners in supporting our adoptive families. We raised $250,000 for the cause of adoption, and now, from that fund, we can cover 25 percent of each family's total adoption costs when they step forward.

Last, adoptive families need support with everyday tangible needs—car seats, baby clothes, and formula, among other things. Babysitting other children while parents attend court appointments for an adopted or foster child is another practical way to help. In cases of international adoption, families often must live in their child's home country for several weeks. During that time, someone needs to take care of their yard, check on their house, and handle daily tasks. Likewise, families adopting from the foster care system often have countless meetings and court dates. It's crucial for Rope Holders to step in and provide support when foster families are consumed with appointments and legal proceedings.

There are a thousand ways that churches can set up adoptive families for success by surrounding them with support. The key is to remember that adoptive families are preparing for spiritual warfare, and they need others who will stand with them in their corner. Don't send adoptive families into the hottest part of the battle alone! If you're interested in how a church can implement a simple structure for holding the rope, see appendix A.

There is one aspect of the adoption process that we haven't discussed: handling fear about adoption. We will turn our attention there in the next chapter.

REFLECTION QUESTIONS

- Whether you will ever adopt or not, how has God gifted you to support people who do?
- In what ways could your local church be more supportive of adoptive families within your congregation?
- How could you change your prayer life to help meet the needs of adoptive families?

9

The Courage of Adoption

~

If you're reading this book, it's likely because you have an interest in Christian adoption or know someone who does. Maybe you're actively considering adoption yourself, or perhaps your church is stepping into these waters. You might already be an adoptive parent, contemplating whether to reenter the spiritual battlefield for another tour. I know dozens of families in that situation. They are thinking about it, but they haven't decided. If you are in that situation, you are standing on the edge of a courageous step of faith. Will you take the step?

Although not everyone is called to adoption, it seems to me that more Christians should adopt than currently do. You may feel the tug on your heart but haven't fully committed. Sadly, many believers get to that point only to pull the plug and deflate the dream. They pray about it, involve their community group in prayer, and talk about it endlessly. They consume books and podcasts, but in the end, many never take the step. Instead, they remain standing on the bank, hesitant to get their feet wet.

When God's people were called to cross the Jordan, it was a dangerous time for a river crossing. The waters raged during the harvest season, but in Joshua 3, God commanded them to step into the river *before* he parted it. In other words, as Mercy Hill pastor Bobby Herrington has stated, "They had to get their feet wet before they could walk on dry ground." Imagine the tremendous courage it must have taken to step into those raging waters with nothing but God's Word to guide them. Yet, empowered by the fear-crushing presence of God, they took that step in faith.

Why do so many Christians stand on the bank of the adoption waters without ever stepping in? Unfortunately, the answer is plain and simple: They succumb to fear. Fear holds us back from fully committing to the purposes and plans God has for us. Every believer has works ordained by God from the foundation of the world, but those works are often scary and daunting. Adoption, like many of God's callings, requires courageous faith—faith that only God can create within us. We need him to crush our fears so we can take the step he's calling us to.

If you didn't fear adoption before reading this book, you probably do now. I've tried to be honest about the spiritual warfare and hardships that come with adoption. It's natural to feel overwhelmed when you consider the financial strain adoption might place on your family. You might worry about the long-term impact that bringing an adopted child into your home could have on your other children. There's also a sense of dread in knowing that adoption stirs up spiritual warfare, with no way of predicting how those challenges will manifest or unfold.

Or maybe you're simply wondering, *Do I have what it takes to do this?* One time, while I was floating down the New River with my kids in inner tubes, a huge storm came out of nowhere.

It felt like a category five hurricane hit us with wind, rain, and, you guessed it, lightning. So we got off the river and took shelter under a tree. We sat there freezing, waiting for who knows what.

About that time, a woman in a kayak came straight toward us. She reached us on the side of the river and asked if we needed help. Of course we did! "Do you have a phone?" I asked. She answered no. "Do you have a rope for the tubes?" I asked. She answered no. "Do you have a towel?" I asked. She answered no. I thought for a moment and finally asked, "Do you have any bottled water?" Yet again, she answered no. "Ma'am," I asked, "what exactly were you envisioning here?" She paused for a moment and said, "Yeah, I'm not really sure, but good luck!" Then she paddled away!

I think many people could compare themselves to that woman on the water. We want to be involved, we want to help with the mission, but we don't have the resources or ability to make a real difference. However, that's not the end of our story! Our God takes what we have and makes it enough. He uses our backgrounds, our unique wiring, our talents, and our spiritual gifts to prepare us for the works he has planned for us. We have what it takes!

Even with all those resources, fear can hold us back from taking the next step. But that doesn't need to be the case, because we have God's presence that crushes fear and instills courage. His presence puts his steel, his power, and his strength into our backbones. Isaiah 40:29 reminds us, "He gives power to the faint, and to him who has no might he increases strength."

God is good and promises us in Romans 8:28 that all things work together for our good. That means that whatever happens, even if we don't understand it, is for our good. When God is with us, we have the most powerful force in the universe on our side! There is nothing he cannot accomplish.

Make no mistake—fear needs to be crushed. We aren't called to make friends with it, manage it, tolerate it, or make peace with it. We want to see fear crushed, destroyed, and completely eradicated from our lives. In the 2006 movie *Talladega Nights: The Ballad of Ricky Bobby*, a race car driver becomes too afraid to drive again after a horrible crash. His absent father reappears in his life, trying to help him overcome his fear. At one point, his father says, "Basically, what happened to you is that you saw the fear. So, before you can even think about any real drivin', you gotta make friends with that fear."[1] His solution? He captures a live cougar, keeps it in a motel bathroom living off old pizza, and then puts the cougar in the car, forcing Ricky Bobby to drive with it! This hilarious scene is the exact opposite of the Christian approach to fear. Again, we aren't called to make friends with fear or simply manage it. Instead, we want God to give us courage to move forward despite our fears as we believe by faith that he will be with us every step of the way.

From a worldly perspective, there's plenty to fear in adoption. But God has not given us a spirit of fear (2 Timothy 1:7). That doesn't mean we never feel afraid or wrestle with fear. It means that, as Christians, we turn all our fears over to Jesus, who has promised to never leave us or forsake us (Hebrews 13:5).

BE STRONG AND COURAGEOUS

The children of Israel faced a scary time when Moses died. Not only was this generational leader gone, but they were heading into a promised land filled with warriors and giants. Despite all of this, God led them away from fear and toward courage (Joshua 1:1–5).

There's no doubt that the people of God faced a serious situation. But serious situations often provide the best opportunities to build faith. Our greatest moments of fear can become our greatest opportunities for growth. No one wants to go through frightening experiences or face stress and turmoil, and yet these challenges are the gymnasium where faith is built. Pastor Bryan Loritts put it this way: "If you are going to get strong, you must pick up things that are heavy."[2] And just as getting physically stronger requires lifting heavy things, growing in faith requires facing weighty challenges.

When we are afraid and turn to Jesus, asking for the gift of faith, we experience firsthand the truth of God's promises. Even when things don't go according to our plans, he is with us and never leaves us. I hope you don't miss the opportunity to witness God's work to build your faith through your adoption. Is it scary? Absolutely. Is much of the future unknown? Yes. But that uncertainty places us in a position to trust God even more.

God calls his people to be strong and courageous. He says, "Do not be frightened" (Joshua 1:9). You don't say these things to someone unless they're about to face a situation where fear is the natural response. For instance, I don't tell my kids to be strong and courageous when they're going to a friend's house they've visited a dozen times. When we're sitting around at night watching *Little House on the Prairie* and my kids ask if they can get ice cream, I never think to say, "Child, as you journey into the kitchen to take possession of the mint chocolate chip, be strong and courageous, and do not be frightened!"

You tell kids to be courageous when they're going to need courage—like when they face live pitching for the first time, get a shot at the doctor's office, or head into a new school. For all the reasons we've discussed in this book, adoption belongs among circumstances that require courage. It's going to be hard, there will be struggles, and fear will naturally arise at times. Maybe fear is even keeping you from taking the next step God is calling you to.

If you're struggling with fear as you read this, these words are for you today: Be strong! Be courageous! Do not be frightened, because God is with you. I don't know exactly how a future adoption will work out for you. I don't know how your other children will be affected. And while I've never personally seen an adoption go unfunded, I can't say how the money will come together. But here's what I do know: None of those uncertainties is a good enough reason to *do fear*. There is no reason to freeze. There is no reason to sit down in fear, choose to stay in it, or not take it to God. Why? Because God is with you. Your reasons to fear shrink in comparison to the glory of knowing that he is with you and wastes nothing in this world. Romans 8:28 assures us that "for those who love God all things work together for good, for those who are called according to his purpose." Whatever God does will prove to be right in the end. We can trust him. If he is with us in adoption, we can walk forward without fear.

KNOW THE LORD IS WITH YOU

How do we know that God will be with us in the deep waters of adoption? We know this because he went through death for us. Jesus went to the cross so that we who were once outside the family could be brought into the family of God. He died to give us permanent access to his presence. Our own adoption into God's family serves as the greatest reminder that he will not abandon us when we step into the mission of adopting others.

Interestingly, the words from Joshua 1 resurface in Jesus's Great Commission in Matthew 28. There Jesus says, "Go therefore and make disciples of all nations. . . . And behold, I am with you always, to the end of the age" (Matthew 28:19–20). God promises to be with us just as he did the children of Israel and the disciples. As we step into the mission of adoption, God's presence is a fear crusher and a courage instiller. His Spirit resides in us because of the gospel, so we do not need to be afraid! Joshua 1:9 encourages us, "Be strong and courageous. Do not be frightened," and the sentiment is echoed in Psalm 27:1: "The Lord is my light and my salvation; whom shall I fear? The Lord is the stronghold of my life; of whom shall I be afraid?" Philippians 4:6 also reminds us not to be anxious about anything!

All of this boils down to a simple truth from Romans 8:31: "If God is for us, who can be against us?" God's presence is kryptonite to fear. Remember, as 2 Timothy 1:7 tells us, fear is a spirit—it is spiritually grown and must be spiritually eradicated.

We have friends whose adoption was not finalized for more than four years. Imagine what a scary situation that would be. It would be so easy to *do fear* by spending time imagining all the scenarios that could remove your precious child from the home. You could succumb to fear by becoming sick with worry. Instead, these friends put their trust in the Lord, knowing that he was working all things together for their good. I am not saying they never felt afraid, but they committed not to actively engage fear. If fear is keeping you from taking the final step of commitment, I encourage you not to succumb to fear. Believer, you already have what you need to take courageous steps of faith. God is with you, so walk in courage!

What does the book of James say? "I will show you my faith by my works" (2:18). What are we actually going to do? My prayer for this book is that it catalyzes hundreds or even thousands of adoptions. I hope churches mobilize for Christian adoption and find this book useful.

It's easy to hide behind big numbers and the momentum of a movement—I see it in church life all the time. We celebrate the number of baptisms or the planting of a specific number of churches. But, in the end, it comes down to whether individual families engage with the mission. Sure, they might feel connected to the ministry's success just by being around it, but that is not the same as actual participation. The question is, What are you going to do? Every single one of us carries a calling, a purpose, and a destiny. God made you with specific works in mind—works he set forth from the foundation of the world. God has children for you to adopt, and if you don't step forward, they may not be adopted. We have the theological motivation and mandate, but do we have the will?

Let's pray, "God, give us the courage to walk in your calling!" Pray today that fear would flee, courage would come, and God would make the adoption path straight before us.

REFLECTION QUESTIONS

- What tangible fears may be keeping you from adopting?
- How has God's presence given you courage in the past, and how does recounting his faithfulness give you courage to move forward?
- After reading this book, what specific next steps do you believe God is calling you to?

Appendix A
Mercy Hill Church's Rope Holder Playbook

In 1792, as missionary William Carey prepared to leave for modern-day India, he famously told his good friend Andrew Fuller, "I will go down into the pit, if you will hold the rope."[1] Though these words were spoken in the context of international mission work, they are equally applicable to foster care and adoption today. Parents who pursue building families through adoption or restoring families through foster care need support. They need encouragement. They need the body of Christ to hold the rope for them.

Those who hold the rope answer the call to stand in resilient faith alongside families serving on the front lines of foster and adoption ministry. They become a source of life-giving relief and encouragement through the many challenges these families face. The four avenues of rope holding—relationship, resource, respite care, and recharge nights—create a pathway of care that we pray enables the church to support families well and, ultimately, to love vulnerable children well.

THE VISION

Statistically, 30 to 50 percent of foster parents quit fostering each year.[2] While multiple reasons abound, the core cause is often burnout due to a lack of support. And though not everyone can foster or adopt, everyone can help. A family or individual may not be in the right stage of life to provide a home for a child in need, but all can offer tangible support to those serving vulnerable children on the front lines.

At Mercy Hill, our model for providing support for Chosen families materializes in the form of rope holding. Rope holding provides an avenue for the church to become an anchor of solidarity and support for foster and adoptive families. Furthermore, rope holding supplies a pathway for all members of the body of Christ to play a meaningful role in responding to God's call to care for vulnerable children. Several models are available for creating support networks for foster and adoptive families. Our initiative and language of rope holding is just one of them. For further ideas, see Promise686 or peruse the Christian Alliance for Orphans website.

Parents of foster and adopted children need broad and practical support for the entire time they care for their child. Foster parents navigate the unique challenges of caring for children who have experienced trauma, supporting birth parents on their path to reunification, and enduring the stress that comes with the instability of the reunification process. Adoptive parents, regardless of the child's age at adoption, will also inevitably encounter trauma-related challenges as they work to build healthy attachments and nurture their child over the years.

The beauty of God's design for the church is that no one should pursue sacred work alone. When the body of Christ operates as God intends, "it builds itself up in love" (Ephesians 4:16). We do this by imitating Christ, who, as we see in Ephesians 5:2, loved us and gave himself for us as a sacrifice to God. By showing the selflessness of Christ to our Christian family—sacrificing our time, treasure, and comforts to support foster and adoptive families—the church can display to an immeasurable degree the glory and grace of God revealed in the gospel.

THE MODEL

At Mercy Hill, our ministry to adoptive families is called Chosen. We encourage four avenues of rope holding: relationship, resource, respite care, and recharge nights. Let's explore each area:

1. Relationship Rope Holders are a Chosen family's first line of support within the church.
2. Resource Rope Holders are those who can meet practical needs for Chosen families but may lack the bandwidth to be a Relationship Rope Holder.
3. Respite care is short-term care in a licensed foster home.
4. Recharge nights are planned quarterly gatherings and date nights for Chosen parents, facilitated by the church.

RELATIONSHIP ROPE HOLDERS

Every foster and adoptive family requires a Relationship Rope Holder as their first line of support. This is life-on-life care, and

Chosen families should receive consistent, dependable support from their Rope Holder. Often, these individuals already have a preexisting relationship with the Chosen family—perhaps they're in the same community group or serve on the same team—but that's not a requirement. However, given Mercy Hill's multisite model, it's recommended that a Relationship Rope Holder attend the same campus or live geographically close to the family they support.

The ideal Relationship Rope Holder regularly reaches out to Chosen parents with encouragement, prayer, and help processing challenges, or simply to be an intentional listener. Often just being present—whether in person or remotely—can be more valuable than any words you might offer.[3] On a secondary level, the Rope Holder is encouraged to spend time with the Chosen family if the parents desire. This could include hosting or providing meals, organizing recreational activities, attending their children's games or performances, and celebrating milestones like birthdays or graduations.

Relationship Rope Holders can also provide childcare for limited periods of time in alignment with the given state's prudent parents standards. For example, North Carolina allows unlicensed homes to care for a foster child for up to seventy-two hours.[4] This means that offering childcare for date nights, court dates, or even a night away is well within the range of offering practical help. Often, foster and adoptive families have more child-related responsibilities than the typical family. There are an increased number of medical appointments, social worker visits, guardian ad litem check-ins, and more. Offering to keep one of their children for just a portion of the day can alleviate logistical stress and be extremely life-giving for the family.

Lastly, Relationship Rope Holders should view their line of support as proactive, not reactive. That won't always be possible, but it should be the goal. An ideal Relationship Rope Holder should have an ongoing idea of the needs of the family so they can extend help without the family having to ask for it.

SUPPORT IDEAS FOR RELATIONSHIP ROPE HOLDERS

- Check in routinely with prayer and encouragement.
- Host meals.
- Provide and/or coordinate meals to take to their home.
- Offer childcare.
- Offer help with drop-offs or pickups.
- Spend intentional time with the family.
- Create care packages.
- Bring coffee on court dates. (Arrive at their door with their favorite hot beverage on the morning of a court date.)
- Help provide basic infant items, if needed (diapers/wipes, car seat, pack and play, etc.).
- Send notes of encouragement (and include gift cards if possible).
- Offer tutoring or mentoring in certain situations.
- Be the person they can call at a moment's notice for urgent needs.

RESOURCE ROPE HOLDERS

As stated earlier, not everyone can foster or adopt, but everyone can help. In the same way, not everyone can be a Relationship Rope Holder, but nearly everyone can be a Resource Rope Holder. Resource Rope Holders may not have the availability or the relational giftings to offer the first-line support of a Relationship Rope Holder, but they can serve Chosen families by meeting practical and tangible needs. These services include meal provision, grocery or store pickups and deliveries, home repairs, or financial gifts to enable special time together.

In sum, if the Relationship Rope Holder is the first line of support for the parent, the Resource Rope Holder serves as a key support for the Relationship Rope Holder. When a Relationship Rope Holder lacks the time, means, or skill set to meet a specific need of the Chosen family, they can rely on a Resource Rope Holder. To facilitate this, an updated database of Resource Rope Holders should be consistently maintained and accessible to everyone in the support network.

The spirit behind rope holding grows out of Romans 12:4–5 and certainly applies to Resource Rope Holders: "For as we have many members in one body, but all the members do not have the same function, so we, being many, are one body in Christ, and individually members of one another" (NKJV). Additionally, Resource Rope Holding can provide those serving with a glimpse into what it looks like to foster or adopt. God may use this experience to stir their hearts toward serving in even deeper capacities.

SUPPORT IDEAS FOR RESOURCE ROPE HOLDERS

- Assist Relationship Rope Holders in all capacities (see above).
- Repair homes.
- Do yard work.
- Maintain or add to the frozen meal stock at the church.

RESPITE CARE

Respite care is short-term care provided to a child who is currently in long-term placement with another foster family. As the name suggests, respite care offers foster parents a break from their responsibilities for a predetermined time. These breaks may be necessary due to travel, medical needs, illness, or simply so that foster parents can take a mental and emotional rest. Respite care can be powerfully life-giving to foster families, often providing them with the rest they need to regain strength and persevere through difficult seasons.

Additionally, the short-term nature of respite care provides an appealing starting point for parents who feel called to long-term foster care but want to test the waters before committing fully. Similarly, respite care is an ideal option for licensed foster parents who wish to continue serving during a season when they lack the availability or capacity to commit to a long-term placement.

KEY FACTS ABOUT RESPITE CARE

- Those providing respite care must be in a fully licensed foster home.
- Most respite placements are for predetermined periods, but sometimes they are not.
- It is important to uphold a schedule and routine similar to that of the long-term foster family in order to assist with a smoother transition to and from homes.

RECHARGE NIGHTS

At Mercy Hill, Recharge Night is an integral part of our annual rhythm to support our Chosen parents. Our vision is to create a space where foster and adoptive parents can pause, catch their breath, and reconnect with each other while sharing time with other parents on a similar journey.

Our recharge nights feature an equipping session focused on a specific theme, such as community, marriage, parenting, or family. The primary goal of this session is to encourage and strengthen Chosen parents in their journey while renewing their vision of foster and adoption ministry through the lens of the gospel. Additionally, the session provides talking points aimed at deepening couples' relationships and ministry, which they can further explore together.

As the capstone of the evening, Mercy Hill partners with local restaurants to provide a date night for each family, offering gift cards for a meal together. Childcare is offered by the church for the entire duration of the event, giving parents a needed break while also allowing volunteers to engage in life-on-life ministry. Additionally, this experience can open doors for volunteers to explore deeper involvement in ministry.

SAMPLE SCHEDULE FOR A RECHARGE NIGHT

5:30 p.m.—Gather, drop off kids at childcare
5:35 p.m.—Welcome and vision casting for the evening
5:40 p.m.—Equipping session
6:00 p.m.—Break for dinner with spouses
8:00 p.m.—Childcare pickup at the church

ROPE HOLDING LOGISTICS AND HELP

There are many considerations in establishing a rope holding ministry at your church. Here are a few suggestions:

1. Designate a point person to assume ownership for rope holding. At Mercy Hill, this role is typically filled by a volunteer.

2. Select Relationship Rope Holders who have a preexisting relationship with their Chosen family, as this increases immediate effectiveness.
3. Use the interest form from Mercy Hill's Chosen (below) to gather information from church members interested in getting involved.
4. Maintain a designated freezer on church property stocked with frozen meals for Chosen families.
5. Host quarterly interest meetings for those seeking to foster, adopt, or become a Rope Holder.

CHOSEN INTEREST FORM

Mercy Hill has an online interest form for church members looking to get involved in our Chosen ministry. Below is the information we ask for on the form.

Form Overview: With the goal of having two hundred adoptive and foster care families in Mercy Hill by 2025, Chosen is about moving followers of Jesus from the sidelines to the front lines of adoption and foster care as well as rope holding. Use this form to let us know who you are and how God might be calling you to build and restore families the way he does!

- name
- email
- phone number
- spouse's name (if applicable)
- campus primarily attended
- ministry of interest: adoption, foster care, Rope Holder

CONCLUSION

Foster and adoption ministry is as hard as it is holy. It is sacred work, and with all sacred work comes the enemy's attack. Denzel Washington once said, "When the devil ignores you, then you know you're doing something wrong."[5] The implication is clear: If you're being attacked, confused, or discouraged by the enemy, it might be a sign that you are doing exactly what God wants you to do. This sentiment likely resonates with many foster and adoptive families. Yet, when faithful servants find themselves in that place, they should never have to go through it alone.

As believers, we have the indwelling of the Holy Spirit and the comfort and help he brings. We have the steadfast love of the Father, in whom we live and move and have our being (Acts 17:28). We have God's Word, which reveals his redemptive plan, his character, and his will for our lives. We have our Savior, Jesus, our redeemer and resurrection life, who lives forever to intercede for us. And we have the church—the body of Christ. In rope holding, the entire body of Christ wraps around foster and adoptive families, joining forces to serve and love vulnerable children.

Appendix B
The Path of Foster Care

We build families through adoption and restore families through foster care. Foster care is an important part of our Chosen ministry at Mercy Hill Church, but it's crucial to understand that foster care is not the same as adoption. While the impulse for Christians to foster comes from the same heart motivation as adoption, the parenting role has distinctly different purposes. God's desire is for families to flourish, but we live in a fallen world where sin and circumstances create broken families. These situations are heartbreaking, but they also present an opportunity for the Christian community to step up and reveal the heart of God to those who are hurting.

God doesn't waste one ounce of suffering in this world. We are told in 1 John 1:5 that "God is light, and in him is no darkness at all." This means that God is not the author of evil, but he does use everything, even bad things, to accomplish his purposes. God is a bit like a judo fighter: He uses the weight of evil against itself to bring about his good plans.

The Baptist network in North Carolina showed a great example of this when Hurricane Helene ripped through the mountains and hollows of Western North Carolina. The devastation was unimaginable. As heartbreaking as the storm was—and as much as it grieved the heart of God to see people suffer—his people were mobilized even before the storm had fully passed. Less than forty-eight hours after the storm hit, churches from all over the state had tractor trailers of supplies heading west. Thousands of volunteers showed up to serve meals and assist with recovery and cleanup efforts. In doing this, they revealed a picture of God's heart for the hurting. It was a sign of a coming kingdom. Likewise, when we step in to adopt or foster, we bring glimpses of a coming kingdom where families are never broken apart and children are never orphaned.

The goal of adoption is to permanently bring a child into a new home, while the goal of fostering is to return a child to their existing home—if it can be made safe. In most cases, this means the biological parents need to make significant changes, but reunification remains the aim. And that is hard. Adoption is hard, as I've discussed, but becoming a foster parent is a different kind of hard. The ministry is tangled in bureaucracy, which can frustrate anyone. Often, foster parents feel like they're working harder to reunite the family than the biological parents. Can you imagine that burden? They have a front-row seat to an overwhelmed system. And ultimately, they enter the process with the expectation that success means their heart will be broken when the child returns home. This is serious stuff. But it's also gospel stuff.

FOSTERING SHOWS SIGNS OF THE KINGDOM

I mentioned a phrase earlier that I think is worth revisiting: *signs of the kingdom*. Bringing signs of the coming kingdom is an effective tool for evangelism. By doing things that align with God's future kingdom, we paint a picture of that reality. In this way, we invite people to explore and consider what God has for them. What if something like fostering children isn't actually building the kingdom, but instead pointing to a kingdom that is coming?

We are told in 1 Peter that we are aliens in this world. Our priorities, thoughts, and actions aren't aligned with citizenship here. We are entirely otherworldly. Part of belonging to a different kingdom means acting like it. When Christians step into fostering children, they are acting as if they are from another world. In that heavenly kingdom, there are no orphaned children and no broken families. So we seek to restore families here because it offers a glimpse of what it will be like there.

Two things are true here. First, when families step into foster care, they are offering a sign of the kingdom that is coming. The houses rebuilt after a flood or disaster won't last forever, but rebuilding them gives a glimpse of a kingdom where people aren't left homeless after a storm. The same applies to foster care. The sign itself isn't the point—but it does signal the greater reality of the coming kingdom.

I don't know if you've ever had the privilege of going to a Buc-ee's travel center and gas station, but trust me, it is a privilege! If there's ever been a symbol of Western opulence and materialism, it's Buc-ee's . . . and it's awesome. This place boasts the largest bathrooms on earth. They chop brisket right in the middle of the store, and you can buy anything there. It's as if Walmart and a Sheetz gas station got married and had a baby, and then that baby married a Tractor Supply and had another baby resulting in Buc-ee's. It's the only store where you can fill up your gas tank, grab a BBQ lunch, and buy a lawn mower, a bag of dog food, and a Christmas tree all in the same visit. Buc-ee's is a whole experience in itself. It's crazy that the signs for Buc-ee's start popping up at least five hundred miles before you arrive.

Imagine a family driving three hundred miles and stopping every time they see a Buc-ee's sign to take pictures and make Instagram reels, all smiles and excitement. But when they finally reach the exit where the Buc-ee's is located, they drive by without stopping. That wouldn't make any sense because they would be paying more attention to the signs than the actual destination.

My silly illustration shows us just how important this third way of thinking is when it comes to signs of the kingdom. On one hand, it would be foolish to say that signs don't provoke desire in the heart. When kids see the Buc-ee's sign, they start begging their parents to stop! Signs of the kingdom of God work in a similar way. Tim Keller used to say something like this: Even if you don't believe in God's kingdom, wouldn't you want it to be true? God's kingdom is a place with no injustice or broken families. It's a place with no sickness, sorrow, death, or tears. When we bring signs of that kingdom to a watching world, our hope is that, for some, it will spark a desire to learn more.

On the other hand, how silly would it be to think that the sign is more important than the kingdom itself? The sign is never the goal; it always points the way to a greater reality, and the same is true with signs of the kingdom. Adoption isn't the point; disaster relief isn't the point; painting a school isn't the point; and restoring families through foster care isn't the point. In fact, any family restored through foster care will again be split apart, by death if by nothing else. But families restored through foster care can most certainly point us to the heart of God and teach people to long for heaven.

FOSTERING PROVOKES DESIRE

Most people want to live in a world where families are not torn apart. Foster care gives Christians a chance to offer a glimpse of that world. There will be no tears at all in heaven. I'm reminded of the end of *The Chronicles of Narnia*, when redemption sweeps across the land and the cry is, "Come further up, come further in!"[1] Matthew 19:28 speaks about the renewal of all things—a sweeping redemption where the new heavens and the new earth invade this world as far as the curse is found. There's also a moment in *The Lord of the Rings* when Samwise Gamgee wakes up, having thought he was doomed, and says, "Gandalf! I thought you were dead! But then I thought I was dead myself. Is everything sad going to come untrue?"[2] Christians believe everything sad is indeed going to come untrue, and that includes the breakup of families.

Therefore, our willingness to enter into foster care carries an evangelistic component. When people see Christians fostering, it can provoke in them a desire for the world that God is bringing. It can also make them wonder who would be willing to pour out their life to see families restored. This is where the evangelistic nature of foster care dovetails with adoption. We've already looked at some of the hardships of adoption and how it raises questions in the minds of unbelievers. The same is true for foster care, and it may create an even greater opportunity to spark curiosity and conversation with unbelievers.

The sacrifice comes in working hard with the hope that the child will eventually leave their home. Foster parents are essentially preparing themselves for heartbreak, and even trauma, because their goal is to see the child reunited with their biological family. I've never known foster parents who didn't experience a deep sense of loss when a child returned home after spending any significant time with them. But they understood that that loss was part of their success.

But don't people foster to adopt? That does happen frequently, and it is a good thing. But for believers, fostering to adopt should only be considered after every attempt at reunification fails. Remember, adoption is a beautiful thing, but it always happens on the heels of the tragedy of family breakup.

In Christian foster care, the upside of permanently bringing a child into your home is not the goal. Instead, the goal is the opposite. Families care for a child, potentially for years, and develop great affection and love for the child. All the while, they hope and pray that one day the child will leave and be reunited with their biological family! The people who do this are aliens—they are living for another kingdom.

FOSTERING IS A MISSION FIELD

Unfortunately, foster care is a dire need nationwide. For example, in my home state, there are currently 11,258 children in out-of-home placements, with only 5,436 licensed foster homes.[3] Ministering through foster care, like adoption, means stepping into the hottest part of spiritual warfare. As you've likely realized by now, Satan loves the breakup of families. Christians who choose to foster are answering a high calling, and in doing so, they bring the light of Christ to three distinct groups of people: foster children, biological parents of foster children, and social workers. This is a robust ministry. Foster care is a mission field.

A MISSION TO THE FOSTER CHILD

Obviously, foster parents minister to the child who has been removed from their home. Can you imagine how vulnerable and confused these children must feel when they are taken from their parents? In 2008, Anna and I became licensed to foster, and as part of our training, we had to try to put ourselves in the shoes of a foster child. Many of these children have experienced abuse and neglect—after all, foster children are removed from their home for a particular reason. In addition to that trauma, they now face the pain of displacement. Everything in a foster child's life is turned upside down in an instant.

Foster parents often meet foster children after what is likely one of the worst days of the child's life. That's hard, but it's exactly what foster parents sign up for. Amid that chaos, they have the opportunity to pour out the love of Christ. Christian foster parents focus first and foremost on ministering to a child experiencing profound brokenness. Part of this ministry involves bringing these children into the rhythms of Christian community and practices for however long they are in the home. A Christian family has a culture of faith before a foster child enters their home, and that culture continues after the child leaves. So while the child is present, the family continues to practice their faith naturally through Bible reading, prayer, and Christian community.

A MISSION TO THE BIOLOGICAL PARENTS

Foster parents also have a mission field with the biological parents of children placed in their care. Often, foster parents and biological parents have an adversarial relationship. Foster parents may feel that the biological parents aren't trying hard enough to keep their families together, while biological parents may be suspicious of foster parents' motives, wondering whether they want to raise the child as their own. These dynamics are challenging.

However, in our church, the best foster parents begin with this crucial presupposition: If the biological parents can't grow and heal, then there is no hope for reunification. In other words, fostering is about ministering to parents and children. So foster parents work hard to maintain open lines of communication. They aim to make it clear to the child's biological parents that they are for them and, tactfully and when appropriate, offer gentle guidance on how to better care for their children. Is this easy? Not at all. Does it always result in a harmonious relationship? Certainly not. But this is the heart posture of a Christian foster family.

Multiple families in our church have developed this kind of relationship with their foster children's families. One family fostered a child for several years and continued working alongside the child's biological parents despite numerous setbacks. In this case, the biological father was committed to doing the hard work required to reunite with his child. The foster father stepped in to mentor him in essential life skills. Now that reunification has occurred, the biological father continues to rely on the foster family as a resource as he raises his child.

Another story comes to mind with a different outcome. A foster family in our church worked tirelessly to pursue reunification for their foster child. To say they went above and beyond would be a colossal understatement. I watched as this family begged God for the salvation of the child's biological parents. They also invested practically, mentoring and offering support to the parents in hopes of reunification. However, in the end, the biological parents didn't lean in, and their parental rights were terminated. It was a devastating outcome. But regardless of the results, it was undeniable that these foster parents had hearts for the child's parents.

A MISSION TO THE SOCIAL WORKERS

Last, Christian foster parents have a mission field with the social workers who manage these challenging cases. Social workers are often overwhelmed by their caseloads, with new cases pouring in constantly. At our church, we've seen that sustained care over time can help develop meaningful relationships with the local foster care system. Many of our foster families regularly invite social workers into our church and look for practical ways to minister to them. These efforts do not go unnoticed.

We've developed a partnership with the local Department of Social Services (DSS), offering a class for parents who have either lost custody of their children or are at risk of losing them. The class, called "Families Count," is intentionally designed to be the most desirable option available to these parents. We provide transportation for parents to and from each class. During the class, a volunteer team serves a homemade meal, and the parents leave with a to-go meal for later. We also offer childcare to ensure they can participate fully. Most importantly, the class is thoroughly gospel-centered. This ministry wouldn't be possible without the relationships built between our foster families and the social workers they've connected with. Because of those relationships, DSS has approved "Families Count" as an option for these families, and with every session, more and more families are attending. In addition to shining the light of Christ on foster children and their biological parents, we also want to walk with social workers through these difficult situations.

Restoring families through foster care is a vital part of the mission. Our prayer is that churches will cast a big vision for their members to be involved. Our Chosen ministry has compiled the data, and in our county, we need two hundred more foster families to match the number of children in the system. I would think the church should produce double the number of families for children that need them. In fact, we long for the day when there are way more families equipped and ready than there are children waiting. In this same county, there are more than five hundred churches! What if every church supported just one licensed family? There is a huge opportunity for the church to be the hands and feet of Jesus and live out the mission of defending the fatherless and visiting the orphan through the ministry of foster care.

Appendix C

Adoption and Foster Care Sermon Series

Pastors, I want to encourage you to consider preaching a series specifically around the ministry of adoption and foster care in your church. Our church did this in 2020, and it was truly catalytic. It sparked a movement that led to setting bold goals for hundreds of families to step off the sidelines and engage in our Chosen ministry. This series not only brought families into the front lines of adoption and foster care, but it also encouraged others to become supportive Rope Holders. The series was instrumental in igniting huge goals, and it changed the culture of our church.

As we explored the heart of God regarding adoption, foster care, fatherlessness, and caring for orphans, our church was deeply blessed, and I know yours will be too. I believe people are naturally drawn to these ministries because something in all of us remembers what it was like to be an outsider. We remember what it was like to be spiritual orphans—strangers outside the covenant of God. The gospel brought us in, and that ignites our hearts for those in similar situations like nothing else can.

What if our churches came together to empty the foster care systems in our states? What if we got serious about building families the way God builds his? Imagine looking around your church one day and seeing dozens, if not hundreds, of children who were chosen to be in the faith family—not just born into it. It's a powerful vision, and I encourage you to dwell on it. Below, you'll find an outline of the six-week Chosen sermon series we did at Mercy Hill Church. If you are a pastor looking for a way to introduce adoption ministry to your congregation or you are a local church member looking to do a Bible study, feel free to pull from these resources for ideas.

CHOSEN SERMON SERIES

WEEK ONE

- Sermon title: "Awe Over Adoption"
- Sermon Scripture: 1 John 3:1–3
- Sermon big idea: Christians are reborn into the family of God. We are children of God because he called us his children.
- Watch online: https://mercyhillchurch.com/media/awe-over-adoption-1-john-3-1-3/

WEEK TWO

- Sermon title: "Fully in the Family"
- Sermon Scripture: Galatians 4:1–7
- Sermon big idea: As the children of God, we are given every right and blessing that comes with being family (inheritance).

- Watch online: https://mercyhillchurch.com/media/fully-in-the-family-galatians-4-1-7/

WEEK THREE

- Sermon title: "What Childlike Faith Really Means"
- Sermon Scripture: Matthew 18:1–6
- Sermon big idea: Childlike faith begins with the awareness of great need.
- Watch online: https://mercyhillchurch.com/media/what-childlike-faith-really-means-matthew-18-1-6/

WEEK FOUR

- Sermon title: "Christianity and Abortion"
- Sermon Scripture: Jeremiah 1:5
- Sermon big idea: The Church stands for life because God forms life.
- Watch online: https://mercyhillchurch.com/media/christianity-and-abortion-jeremiah-1-5/

WEEK FIVE

- Sermon title: "Plan and Purpose"
- Sermon Scripture: Esther 4:14
- Sermon big idea: God has a plan for every vulnerable child.
- Watch online: https://mercyhillchurch.com/media/plan-purpose-esther-4-14/

WEEK SIX

- Sermon title: "True Religion"
- Sermon Scripture: James 1:22–27

- Sermon big idea: Caring for the vulnerable is a demonstration of faith.
- Watch online: https://mercyhillchurch.com/media/true-religion-james-1-22-27/

Endnotes

CHAPTER 1

1. The Annie E. Casey Foundation, "Child Welfare and Foster Care Statistics" (blog), July 27, 2024, https://www.aecf.org/blog/child-welfare-and-foster-care-statistics.

2. "KIDS COUNT Data Center from the Annie E. Casey Foundation," n.d., https://datacenter.aecf.org/.

3. Adoption and Foster Care Analysis and Reporting System, "The AFCARS Report Preliminary FY 2015 Estimates as of June 2016, No. 23," U.S. Department of Health and Human Services, Administration for Children and Families, Administration on Children, Youth and Families, Children's Bureau, https://bettercarenetwork.org/sites/default/files/afcarsreport23.pdf.

4. Christian Alliance for Orphans, "Statistics (Orphan Care)," August 30, 2023, https://cafo.org/orphan-care-statistics/.

CHAPTER 3

1. Elisabeth Elliot, quoted in *Elisabeth Elliot Quotes About Sacrifice*, *AZQuotes*, accessed August 6, 2025, https://www.azquotes.com/author/17940-Elisabeth_Elliot/tag/sacrifice.

2. J. D. Greear, "A Whole New Kind of Obedience: Jonah 4:1–11" (Sermon), The Summit Church, January 29, 2012. Accessed July 21, 2025. https://summitchurch.com/message/a-whole-new-kind-of-obedience-jonah-41-11.

3. Robert Barron, *2 Samuel*, Brazos Theological Commentary on the Bible (Brazos Press, 2015), 39.

4. Barron, *2 Samuel*, 87.

CHAPTER 4

1. See Tony Merida and Rick Morton, *Orphanology: Awakening to Gospel-Centered Adoption and Orphan Care* (New Hope Publishers, 2011).

CHAPTER 5

1. Timothy Keller, *Center Church: Doing Balanced, Gospel-Centered Ministry in Your City* (Zondervan, 2012), 67.

2. Wikipedia, "Secretariat (horse)," October 14, 2024. https://en.wikipedia.org/wiki/Secretariat_(horse)#Belmont_Stakes.

3. Bob Ehalt, "Anderson's Tremendous Belmont Call Stands Test of Time," *BloodHorse*, June 6, 2023, https://www.bloodhorse.com/horse-racing/articles/269193/andersons-tremendous-belmont-call-stands-test-of-time.

CHAPTER 6

1. Tony Merida, "1 Reason Why We Adopt: Theology," *Lifeway*, accessed July 21, 2025, https://www.lifeway.com/articles/the-reason-we-adopt-by-tony-merida.

2. John Piper, "Inspired by the Incredible Early Church," *Desiring God*, April 6, 1994, https://www.desiringgod.org/articles/inspired-by-the-incredible-early-church.

CHAPTER 8

1. Cornerstone International, "Will You Hold the Rope?" accessed August 6, 2025, https://cornerstoneinternational.org/vision-video/.

2 John Piper, "*The Weapon Serves the Wielding Power*," message delivered January 6, 1985, *Desiring God*, accessed August 6, 2025, https://www.desiringgod.org/messages/the-weapon-serves-the-wielding-power.

3. Randy Alcorn, *The Treasure Principle: Unlocking the Secret of Joyful Giving* (Multnomah Publishers, 2001), 18.

CHAPTER 9

1. Adam McKay, dir., *Talladega Nights: The Ballad of Ricky Bobby*, Sony Pictures, August 4, 2006.

2. Bryan Loritts, remarks at The Summit Collaborative Conference, Greensboro, NC, October 5, 2022.

APPENDIX A

1. Nathan Finn, "Who Will Hold the Ropes: A Plea for Great Commission Pastors and Churches," *Church Leaders*, February 19, 2018, https://churchleaders.com/outreach-missions/outreach-missions-articles/319554-will-hold-ropes-plea-great-commission-pastors-churches-nathan-finn.html.

2. Christian Alliance for Orphans, "US Foster Care Statistics 2024: Data & Trends [Updated]," October 21, 2024, https://cafo.org/foster-care-statistics/.

3. Lifeline Children's Services, "Equipped to Love," Facilitator's Guide, Module 1, 2016, https://lifelinechild.org/wp-content/uploads/2021/08/Equipped-to-Love-Module-1.pdf.

4. "Reasonable and prudent parent standard," North Carolina General Assembly, n.d. https://www.ncleg.gov/EnactedLegislation/Statutes/PDF/BySection/Chapter_131D/GS_131D-10.2A.pdf.

5. Denzel Washington, "*When the Devil ignores you, then you know you're doing something wrong*," YouTube short video, 0:30, posted by OutstandingScreenplays, published ca. April 2024, accessed August 6, 2025, https://www.youtube.com/shorts/OO08-qXac-c.

APPENDIX B

1. C. S. Lewis, *The Last Battle,* The Chronicles of Narnia, vol. 7 (HarperCollins Publishers, 2001), 760.

2. J. R. R. Tolkien, *The Return of the King,* The Lord of the Rings, part three (William Morrow, 2012), Kindle edition, chap. 4, "The Field of Cormallen."

3. Christian Alliance for Orphans, "US Foster Care Statistics 2024: Data & Trends [Updated]," October 21, 2024, https://cafo.org/foster-care-statistics/#children-in-foster-careThere.